"When you pick up a book about a "Wild West Cowgirl" you expect an exciting ride, and Diane Helentjaris provides one. Lulu's journey from unassuming Steubenville, Ohio to international renown leads through the brash, colorful world of early 20th century traveling shows, a world that stands in surprising contrast to the stereotypical image of Victorian America. It's an inside view of the uniquely American institution of the Wild West show, and the way these shows commodified two ways of life and the flawed relationship between them.

Helentjaris knows a good story when she sees one and departs from Lulu's trail to introduce us to a cast of fascinating characters swirling around the plucky cowgirl. In the process she uncovers lives lived on the road and in the margins, ferreting out information from diverse sources to paint rich backgrounds and breathe life into her subjects. At the center of it all is the fierce and courageous Lulu, blithely defying so many of the expectations for women of her era, risking life and limb and looking good the whole time - no one could ask for a better heroine. Infused with wry humor, this book is both thought-provoking and a genuinely fun read - a look into rarely-seen corners of American history and a rousing chronicle of a fearless life."

—**Kasey Eichensehr, Senior Curator, Clark County (Ohio) Historical Society**

"I felt myself standing in the room (or corral) with Lulu Bell and the host of characters around her. Helentjaris somehow transported me backwards in time with truly amazing historical detail. Within a few pages, the author's empathy with Lulu's many trials and tribulations comes forward. All are handled with grace and humor."

—**John I. Brown, III, retired FAA Safety Inspector**

"This well-researched and well-written book is a joy to read, especially if you love history. Lulu's story is a page burner. Had I started reading earlier in the day, it would have been a one-sit read."

—**Lenora Rain-Lee Good, author** *Madame Dorion: Her Journey to the Oregon Country*

"Wild West shows haunt our collective idea of the "Old West" with now stereotypical images of cowboys with guns ablaze and lassos spinning; native people cast in the role of marauding Indians; horses galloping at full tilt every which way. For many, this mythic West begins and ends with Buffalo Bill Cody's Wild West show, but this is only a small part of the story. *I Ain't Afraid* uncovers a much more rich and vivid history.

Exploring in-depth the life and adventures of once famous and later forgotten Queen of the Cowgirls Lulu Bell Parr, this book not only relates the biography of a talented tough-as-nails woman with endless pluck, a wild-yet-trusty steed, and countless stunning outfits, but also opens wide the complex and diverse communities that surrounded shows such as Buffalo Bill's, Pawnee Bill's, and the Miller Brothers' 101 Ranch.

Helentjaris's tales of the triumphs and tragedies of Lulu Bell Parr's family, life, and career reveal real western vistas hidden within the mythic one. A West where fame and death were always waiting just around the next corner; a West packed with equal parts opportunity and danger; a West where reinventing yourself is as easy as dusting yourself off, getting back on the horse that just threw you, and riding off to the next adventure. This is a journey well worth taking and a book you won't be able to put down."

—**Laura E. Christiansen, Curator of Manuscripts & Archives, Thomas Balch Library**

I AIN'T AFRAID

THE WORLD OF LULU BELL PARR, WILD WEST COWGIRL

DIANE HELENTJARIS

ALKIRA
PUBLISHING

I Ain't Afraid
The World of Lulu Bell Parr, Wild West Cowgirl
Diane Helentjaris
Copyright © 2024
Published by Alkira Publishing, Australia
ABN: 32736122056
http://www.alkirapublishing.com

All rights reserved. No part of this publication may be reproduced, stored in a retrieval system or transmitted in any form or by any means electronic, mechanical, audio, visual or otherwise, without prior permission of the copyright owner. Nor can it be circulated in any form of binding or cover other than that in which it is published and without similar conditions including this condition being imposed on the subsequent purchaser.

Paperback ISBN: 978-1-922329-70-7
Hardback ISBN: 978-1-922329-72-1

Cover image: Lulu Bell Parr. Object ID# 152b, Buffalo Bill Museum and Grave, Golden, Colorado.

Back cover: A Bevy of Wild West Girls Just as They Appear in the Arena. Poster. Object ID# 73.0694a, Buffalo Bill Museum and Grave, Golden, Colorado.

Lulu Bell Parr. Painting by Brian Whelan. Author's collection.

ALSO BY THE AUTHOR

The Indenture of Ivy O'Neill

"Delightful account…thoroughly enjoyable."
—**Review by the Novel Historical Society.**

"Helentjaris is masterful at weaving stories. She not only gives us diverse and believable characters, she gives them bones and muscle, brains and speech, she clothes them in detail and personalities. Had I read more books like hers when considerably younger, I may have become a serious, educated historian."
—**Lenora Rain Good, Author**

DEDICATION

To Scott Suther, for showing us history is for everybody.

CONTENTS

Foreword	1
Prologue	3
A Hole in the Heart	8
Steubenville	13
Love Comes Calling	23
Dorcas's Origin Story	31
Marrying Time	43
Metamorphosis	47
On the Road	66
The Cowgirl's Life	79
Lulu Finds Her Calling	92
A Rising and Falling Star	97
Interlude	102
The Pluckiest Little Woman	106
Time to Hit the Road	116
Two Bills	122
New Partners	134
Vaudeville Calls	140
Back with the Bills	146
Venice	149
Bring in Your Bad Ones	158
Votes for Women	164
Stardust	176

Thirteen	179
Lulu and the Mulhalls	188
Asea	197
South America	203
Heading Back	206
Be Brave and Go Like a Man	215
The Tried-and-True Blue	221
The Cowboy Boxer	231
The Optimistic Heart	235
Time for Tiger Skin and the Tantlingers	240
Back to Britain and Beyond	244
Clowning Around	256
Still at It	265
Déjà Vu	271
Brother Bill	274
Riverside Remembrances	282
Fetching the Water	286
Epilogue	290
Acknowledgments	299
Bibliography	301
About the author	306

FOREWORD

I am deeply indebted to present-day technology for making this book possible. Advances in sharing information which have made research not only easier, but also more pleasant. As a celebrity, Lulu Bell Parr left behind innumerable newspaper mentions from her heyday. These digitized records, available through free public sources as well as paid services, made tracing her path possible. Of course, as a performer in an industry prone to fantasy and exaggeration, Lulu's newspaper coverage was often not exactly true — entertaining, with bits of reality, but not always accurate.

Indigenous people are an important part of Lulu and her family's story. Today, in the United States, there is no agreement on nomenclature for the Indigenous. I have chosen to use the term "Native American" when the Indigenous individual's tribe is unclear.

"Life is a daring adventure or nothing."
—Helen Keller

PROLOGUE

Medway, Ohio
1961

At eleven, I ran away from home. I fled our white ranch house with the pink shutters and fast-walked through Schauer Acres. The plat of newish one-story homes edged Medway, a hamlet fifteen miles northeast of Dayton, Ohio. Medway had no stoplights, no local government, and few people. Life revolved around farming and nearby Wright-Patterson Air Force Base.

My mother had, for the first time in my life, taken a job. She was gone to the Air Force base all day and took her cool grace and calmness with her. No longer could I pepper her with questions and chatter as she glided around the kitchen. No longer did the aroma of cinnamon-laced bread pudding fill the afternoon hours. Mom didn't stand out in the backyard, reach into a cotton bag on a hanger for a wooden clothespin, and hang the sheets to dry. She no longer ironed Dad's hankies into precisely-folded squares nor our hand-embroidered pillowcases into smooth rectangles. Gone. She was gone, only home at night and on weekends.

In her place, yet not replacing her, came a string of babysitters. My rambunctious brothers and I ran through six sitters in the first year of Mom's employment.

One fine summer's day, disgusted with our current babysitter, the meanest and laziest of the half dozen, I left home with no destination in mind. I should have learned from my cousin David. He'd recently run away at age five. Little David wisely packed Oreos in his Red Flyer wagon for the jaunt around the block. I took nothing.

The afternoon was hot and clear. No one else was outdoors. The sun warmed my shoulders and threatened a sunburn. I passed my friend Debbie Wadovsky's brick house, then crossed Lower Valley Pike, and reached the Medway Cemetery.

Medway Cemetery. 2021. Photograph by author.

I liked to go to the cemetery and nose around the

gravestones surrounding the old brick Mennonite church. Not all the burials were of Mennonites. My favorite featured an embedded turn-of-the-twentieth-century photograph of a pretty woman with her dark hair piled up on her head. How the photograph remained unscarred by rain and snow mystified me.

I lay down in the tall timothy grass edging the graveyard, in the spot where the horses had once stomped their hooves, awaiting the end of church service. My friend Mary Ellen's dad often lumbered down Lower Valley in his tractor, traveling from one field to another. His brimmed black hat rode high over traffic from his seat atop the tractor. He was not the type to interfere with another. Drivers in cars couldn't see me nestled in the grass. I felt safe. A breeze carried the aroma of turned soil. My mind wandered. I dozed off.

Within an hour, my dark mood dissipated. Dinner at home beckoned more than the open road. I stood up, brushed a few stems of timothy from my shorts, and walked home past the quiet houses dozing in the sun.

From her perch on the back stoop, the babysitter eyed me as I crossed the yard. She took a drag off her cigarette, blew silver smoke straight up over her face, flicked the ash onto the grass, then mumbled a desultory, "What were y'all doin'?" She was, of course, more than satisfied with my answer of "nothing."

Unknown to me, while I had napped in the graveyard, Wild West cowgirl Lulu Bell Parr snoozed in eternal rest a few feet away. Lulu Bell Parr, who performed before royalty, thrilled thousands, traveled the world — "lady bucking horse riding champion of the world" — was buried in an unmarked grave in the Medway Cemetery.

For a few years, before our family moved out to Medway,

I Ain't Afraid

my life and Lulu Bell's had overlapped in time and location. Lulu Bell had lived fewer than three miles away—across the Mad River from my Dayton home, amid her Wild West mementos.

At a time when my father was teaching me Annie Oakley's birth name and driving me up to North Star, Ohio to see her grave, Lulu Bell still remembered her friendship with Annie. I twirled my silver cap gun and thrilled to my first pair of cowgirl boots, but Lulu had a gift gun from Buffalo Bill stowed in her dirt-floored home. I treasured my autographed photo from singing cowboy Kenny Roberts, but Lulu owned entire albums stuffed with Wild West memories. She would have known why I begged for a pony.

Diane Helentjaris, age 3. Author's collection.

Lulu Bell Parr was brave. She thirsted for independence. She understood the allure of the West as a pathway to selfhood. I would have been encouraged as an eleven-year-old runaway to know her story, to learn how she escaped the ennui of tiny towns and the constraints of thinking small.

Lulu Bell Parr's story remained buried with her bones until the early 2000s. Here is what I have unearthed.

A HOLE IN THE HEART

Fort Wayne, Indiana
1876

There's a hole in the heart of the abandoned child. A lifelong hole, an abyss. Though the fragmentation of Lulu Bell Parr's family left an indelible footprint, time has erased the precise dates her parents walked out. She was old enough to feel the shame of being left behind and too young to escape the damage.

Few facts pin themselves to Lulu's early life. Everyone who's ever voiced an opinion agrees she was born in Fort Wayne, Indiana, on November 14 or maybe it was November 11, but certainly in 1876. She later claimed to be a girl of the West, the frontier. In one respect, she was. In the past, Indiana had been the frontier, the borderland, the West — created as a domicile for Native Americans pushed off their lands in the East. Fort Wayne had existed only thirty years at the time of Lulu's birth. Earlier on, known as Kekionga, the site was the capital of the Miami nation.

Whether a Westerner or Midwesterner, Lulu was often called "Lula" by her friends and relatives. She came from a small family. Her parents, William H. Parr and Elizabeth Ann Myers Parr only stayed together long enough to create two children, Lulu and her brother, William Alfred Parr, nicknamed "Willie." He was born four years before her in Oakdale, Pennsylvania, near Pittsburgh.

By 1880, Lizzie — as Elizabeth Parr was known — and her children were living outside of Toledo with a James Parr, who may have been Lizzie's brother-in-law. James Parr worked at Milburn Wagon Company. William H. Parr, described as a carpenter, also worked at Milburn Wagon Company, but bunked at Milburn House, hinting at a marital split.

Eventually, both parents discarded the children, as if they were a worn-out umbrella or a broken pencil. Neither Parr nor William were rare names in the region, making it easy for Lulu's father to fade to obscurity. He was claimed to have wandered off to the West — though the West might have been anywhere from Illinois to California or Washington or just plain anywhere west of his family. Lizzie moseyed back to her hometown of Steubenville, Ohio.

I Ain't Afraid

Encampment of Pawnee Indians at Sunset, 1861/1869 by George Catlin. Courtesy National Gallery of Art.

    Lulu and her brother were left in the care of their uncle (or at least they called him their uncle), the saintly William Patton Sheehan. Sheehan had lived down the street from William H. Parr in 1878. That same year, he had also been a clerk and William H. Parr a laborer at a carriage company, Coombs and Company. Sheehan's wife, Jennie, was a Parr, but how or even if, she was connected to William Parr is unclear.

    Sheehan was a fine man, a farmer turned railroad worker, with solid gold personal habits – a conductor everyone on the train knew and liked, a worker admired by his peers, a loving father to his daughter Lillian, and a good husband to his wife Martha Jane "Jennie." A local history describes him as "a well-known and popular citizen and successful in business." He and Jennie were the kind of couple who evoked the thought that maybe it would have been better if they had always parented Lulu and Willie and, barring that, if they could at least raise the little ones to adulthood. But life rarely follows the preferred script.

Somehow, someway Jennie Sheehan lost her health. After being sick for four months, in February 1885, she was thought to be recovering. By March, she was "slowly recovering from a serious illness" at her sister Mrs. William Ross's home in Dayton, Ohio. But the bottom dropped out. On June 8, 1885, thirty-six-year-old Jennie died at home in Fort Wayne.

Jennie was eulogized as "a most amiable woman and was warmly loved by her friends. She had been sick for some time but was believed to be convalescing lately." Her death was attributed to spinal disease. The attendance was "very large" at her funeral and the cortege of carriages long. She left behind her fifteen-year-old daughter Lillian and her husband. Her widower, William, soldiered on as a train conductor.

Lulu, age nine, and Willie, thirteen, once again faced the loss of a parental figure. Lulu later said her formal education stopped at the third grade; Willie, at the fourth. It is likely their time with the Sheehans, as well as their formal education, collapsed with Jennie's failing health and death.

Lulu's origins and most of her childhood are misty. Lulu made up fantastical stories, swirling with drama and pathos. According to one tale, her parents were homesteaders on the frontier. She spun fanciful yarns of growing up on her father's ranch out West. The location changed with the telling,

I Ain't Afraid

moving from Wyoming to Oklahoma or Nebraska.

    She often killed her parents off when she spoke of her childhood, at times in the goriest way. In one version of her early life, she came from wealth, was orphaned at eight, and raised by her cousin, Buffalo Bill Cody. In that fable, she added the unnecessary fillip of every single relative of hers, except Buffalo Bill, being dead as well – grandparents, brothers, and sisters. In an especially detailed whopper, she remembered taking her father his lunch pail at age ten as he toiled in a Texas railroad yard, then recounted his death by a steam locomotive. Anything was better than exposing her vulnerability and the pain of being cast aside.

STEUBENVILLE

Steubenville, Ohio
1894

Despite whatever adventures befell them after they left the shelter of the Sheehans, Lulu and her brother survived. Willie grew up to be Bill, a man about five feet ten inches in height who earned his living with his hands and his back. Eventually, he centered his young adulthood around Steubenville and kept in touch with his mother.

Lulu blossomed into a striking beauty. Her wide mouth, square jaw, and even features were topped by a pile of dark blonde hair. She was petite, with a delicacy that offset her natural athleticism. Lulu knocked back attention from others as if it were whiskey and she, an alcoholic. Though she yearned to be a performer, she held herself aloof in the day-to-day world. She was a loner. The sort of girl who does better with animals than people. She loved horses. In later years, a newspaper reporter spoke with Lulu.

> *She learned to ride, she says, when her father placed her on an untamed pony and told her to stay there or be punished. "I was more scared of my father than of the pony," Miss Parr relates, "so I stayed."*

I Ain't Afraid

At eighteen, after a sojourn out West with her father, Lulu moved in with her mother in Steubenville. The town lay in a natural amphitheater on the west bank of the Ohio River. Rolling hills, the shoulders of the Appalachian Mountains, pressed against its eastern edges. A seediness clung to Steubenville, as it did to the other towns strung like dirty freshwater pearls along the Mississippi River basin. For generations, the brown river washed up evil along with the good — peddlers and preachers, businessmen and crooks.

Bird's Eye View, Steubenville, Ohio. Postcard. Author's collection.

The Ohio River had comfortably fed, clothed, and educated Lulu's mother, Lizzie, and her three siblings as they grew up. By 1860, Lulu's grandfather, at age forty-one, declared ownership of real estate worth eight-thousand dollars and a personal estate of seven hundred dollars. His two daughters, Emma and Elizabeth Ann (Lulu's mother

Lizzie), and his son were educated. Elizabeth Ann attended school through at least age seventeen.

Though brought up on a farm, Lulu's grandfather, George H. Myers, was a steamboat captain with a home in town. He piloted paddlewheelers as far as New Orleans. More than twenty men from the town made their living as captains during the heyday of steamboat travel. During the Civil War, Myers served the Union cause ferrying men and goods up and down the Ohio, the Mississippi, and their tributaries.

Steubenville was prominent in the steamboat industry, though the start was rocky. The first steamboat to float out of a Steubenville boatyard was the *Bazaleel Well*. A joint venture, one firm built the cabin and hull; another, the boiler and engine.

Things did not go well. As the boat puffed upriver for Pittsburgh, a pump failed. The passengers were enlisted to help keep the boat afloat by filling buckets with river water. By the second day, they had made four miles; by the third day, the bells of the churches in Steubenville were still heard. The *Bazaleel Well* ran out of fuel. Fenceposts were cut up and burned. A wagonload of coal was ordered, but someone released "a puff of steam…from the safety valve" and frightened the horses pulling the cart of coal. They bolted and scattered the fuel over a ten-acre cornfield. The unfortunate passengers pitched in again, gathering the lumps of coal. Eventually, the *Bazaleel Well* reached Pittsburgh.

Despite the rough beginning, another sixteen ships would originate in Steubenville, an industry that would not fade until the 1870s with the rise of railroads.

I Ain't Afraid

View of Steubenville, Ohio. (circa 1851 – 1859) *Gleason's Pictorial Drawing Room Companion*, page 185. Author's collection.

In 1894, Lulu and Lizzie lived in a modest frame duplex at 617 Adams Street. Next door a "mom and pop" grocery store sold a hodgepodge of tinned foods and sundries. Day and night, the rattle and clatter of trains a block away on the Panhandle Railroad tracks, punctuated their life.

Lulu's spry, eighty-one-year-old grandmother Dorcas Myers was part of their life as well.

There was no aura of prosperity in Lulu's life. The three women barely scrabbled together enough money to get by. Like other widows of Civil War veterans, Dorcas received a monthly pension of twenty dollars on behalf of George

Myers' service after his 1885 death.

Lizzie, in her forties, earned a precarious living at society's margins. She was a fortune teller, a seer, in a profession for the desperate by the equally desperate. Rolled up in the tradition of witchcraft, strong disapproval hammered it in the early days of the American Colonies. Soothsaying was a felony in Virginia. Practitioners risked punishment by ducking, which could be fatal. Ducking involved binding the accused and tossing them into a body of water. If they floated, they were considered guilty. If they sank, innocent. Those who sank risked dying if not retrieved in time. Or, instead of spending the time ducking the accused witches, they could be directly put to death.

In New England, fortunetelling was dealt with as a religious matter and the Bible had clear taboos against it. With the horrific loss of men in the Civil War, interest rose in communicating with the dead. Even the White House became the site of seances as Mary Lincoln attempted to reach her dead children, and later, her assassinated husband.

Lizzie was not the only person eking out a scorned living as a fortune teller in the area. In 1898, a "lawn fete" fundraiser by the First M.E. Church's mission band included a "popular" fortune teller's tent. In 1900, a Madam Landers advertised her business at 309 South 6th Street. She willingly told the past, present, and future. Ladies paid a quarter. Inexplicably, she charged men double, a half dollar a session.

Actress Lillian Russell portraying a fortune teller. 1895. Courtesy Library of Congress.

Fortune tellers might be blamed for any number of problems. A Sandusky man blamed one for encouraging him to transfer ownership of his farmlands. He claimed his fiancée wanted to cheat the children from his first marriage out of their inheritance. In 1903, the Steubenville jail housed a murderer who claimed a fortune teller led him to doubt the faithfulness of his wife.

Lizzie Parr's exact prognostications went undocumented.

Lulu's job opportunities were narrowed by her lack of education, skills, and experience. Yet, at eighteen, she needed to make a living, to feed the family kitty. She followed the career path of many uneducated women and became a domestic servant. Lulu took a job at Mosgrove's New U.S. Hotel.

The brick three-story hotel was nearly a century old. Built in 1798, less than a year after the town was platted, it was a silent witness to decades of history. When Lizzie was sixteen, during the summer of 1866, President Johnson, in a bid to drum up political support, embarked on a whistlestop tour dubbed "Swing Around the Circle." On June 13th, his train chugged into Steubenville.

The Myers family likely knew of the president's visit. They may have joined the three thousand gawkers milling about the corner of High and Market Streets, looking up in anticipation at the balcony of Mosgrove's New U.S. Hotel.

Johnson had brought along a cadre of heavy hitters — General Ulysses S. Grant, Admiral Farragut, and Secretary of State William H. Seward. Locally-born heroes General George Armstrong Custer and Colonel George McCook rounded out the president's team.

To get things rolling, Grant, Custer, and Farragut were introduced from the balcony. The crowd cheered. Next came Johnson. The crowd erupted in groans, hoots, huzzas, and calls for Grant to return.

I Ain't Afraid

Johnson would have none of it. He first chastised his audience with a Bible-inspired "Let them alone; they know not what they do." The taunts and catcalls continued. Johnson next stooped to quoting poetic doggerel and harped a "well-bred man will not insult me." Johnson then left abruptly for his train. Newspapers blamed the disturbance on a group of unruly boys. The *New York Times* reported, "The Reception at Steubenville Not Satisfactory."

The following day, Johnson spoke in Johnstown, Pennsylvania. To accommodate bystanders, a temporary platform had been built over a drained canal. The platform collapsed under the weight of the crowd, plunging men, women, and children twenty feet into the canal bed. Thirteen people died. More than one hundred were injured. The Presidential train, with the President onboard, debarked soon after. Rescue efforts were still underway.

The public reacted with disgust. They were unassuaged by Johnson's donation of five hundred dollars for the injured, his staff who stayed behind to help, and the claim that lingering would have risked collision with other trains. The press excoriated him. "Swing Around the Circle" was a failure and would be served up as fodder in President Andrew Johnson's later impeachment trial.

The Mosgrove's prime location, downtown and snugged up to the Ohio River, kept customers flowing through its door over the years. Steamboat captains strolled the block or two from the wharf to do business at the hotel. As rail transportation shoved steamboats out of the picture, trains rolled in and deposited travelers at not one, but two, nearby passenger depots. Masons met over wine and food in the hotel dining room. Wedding parties toasted new couples. Parties out for a jaunt on the Ohio stopped in for a meal.

An 1896 advertisement in a souvenir album for Buffalo Bill's Wild West Show declared Mosgrove's New U.S. Hotel to be "Strictly first-class. Centrally located. Headquarters for professionals."

Lulu's short walk to work — only four blocks — was the easy part for her. Once she reached the hotel to start her day, things went downhill fast. Over decades of re-dos, make-dos, and add-ons, the hotel's footprint had expanded willy-nilly. Staff sweated and toiled in the first-floor laundry, kitchen, and office. Meanwhile, guests lolled, dreamed up crackpot business deals, rattled newspapers, and swapped jokes in the large social hall, dining room, and reading room.

After a starchy Victorian dinner, overnighters wandered up to their sleeping rooms on the second and third floors. They hoped the heavy meals might act as a sedative. In the sweltering summertime, they yearned for the hotel's windows and high ceilings to entice a breeze over their pillows. But sleep proved elusive in the hot, sticky humidity of the insufferable river valley nights.

No matter where Lulu worked — in the kitchen, dining room, guest rooms, or laundry — the labor was sheer drudgery. Her armpits were often sopping wet. Stinging beads of sweat ran down her forehead and into her eyes. All work was hand work, no matter how delicate the result might appear. Pie meringues were whipped to a froth with a whisk or, even, a fork. Sheets were scrubbed on a knuckle-busting metal and wood washboard and boiled in cauldrons. Irons lived up to their name, manufactured of heavy black iron and heated on a stove. Loads, whether trays of roast meat or baskets of sheets, were cumbersome, arm and back-straining affairs.

I Ain't Afraid

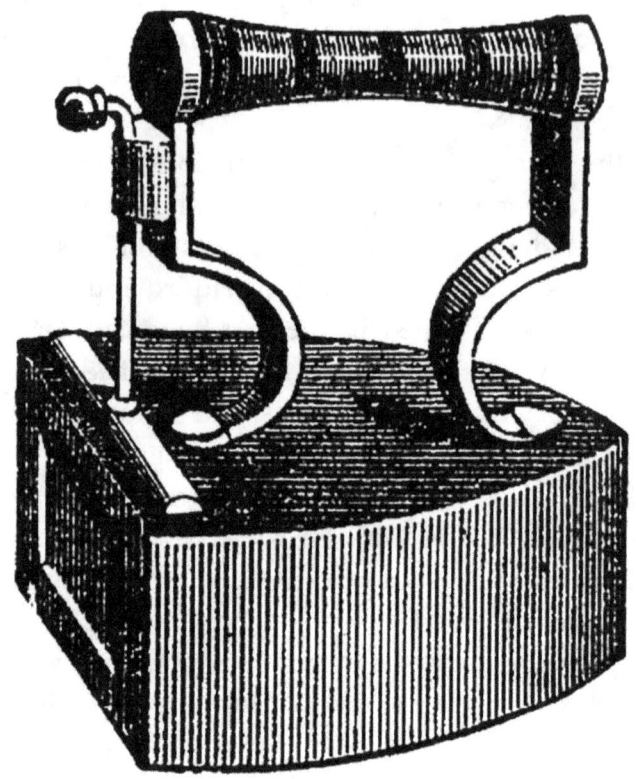

BOX-IRON

Box Iron. Courtesy of the Graphics Fairy.

For her effort, Lulu earned three dollars a week. It was not much money, but Lulu had to take what she could get. Still, she dreamed. One goal was to become a performer. Another was to buy her mother new parlor furniture.

LOVE COMES CALLING

Steubenville, Ohio
1894

Strewn over the nearby hills and valleys, in farmhouses and cottages, was a hodgepodge of Lulu's relatives. Aunts. Uncles. Cousins. All sorts of cousins. Among them was a thirty-two-year-old farmer named Frank Wheaton. Wheaton ranked among Lulu's shirt-tail cousins — one of those minor kin who hung on by the most tenuous of blood ties and carried a whiff of a bad odor.

Frank's grandfather was Lulu's great-uncle. Wheaton farmed west of town, out in an area of Jefferson County which, for a brief few years, claimed a post office and a name — Fernwood. A bachelor, Frank lived with his widowed mother and younger brother. From time to time, he came into Steubenville, Jefferson's county seat. With the assumed entitlement of a single man, he often stopped by Cousin Lizzie's home for a free meal.

Around the time of Lulu's arrival from the West, Frank dropped in at Lizzie's. Lulu wasn't in, but a photograph of her was. Frank took it in hand, said she was pretty, then declared to Lizzie that he "would have her." There was no law against marrying a second cousin and besides, Lulu Bell Parr was gorgeous.

Lizzie snapped, "Frank, I don't think you will."

But Frank was a sly one. With matrimony in mind, he hunkered down to snare his quarry. Like a cowboy after an unbranded calf, step one involved separating the diminutive teenager from her mother. They went on walks and even more to Lulu's liking, rode horses across the countryside.

Frank questioned Lulu about her job at Mosgrove's. How much did it pay? Lulu told him. He vowed to match her hotel wages if she'd come out to his farm and help his mother, Eliza.

Then in her early sixties, Eliza Myers Wheaton had been widowed for nearly twenty years. Frank's brother, in his early twenties, was also unmarried and still at home.

The offer appealed to Lulu. She moved to the Wheaton farm for the winter, about twenty miles from Lizzie's.

Frank failed as an employer. He shorted Lulu each of the three months she was on his farm. The first and second month, Frank paid her nine dollars rather than the twelve he had promised. The third month, he paid her eight dollars. Lulu fled the farm in the spring and returned to her mother.

Undaunted by this bump in the rocky road to romance, Frank pressed his luck with sad results. By September 1895, the cousins were spatting face-to-face over a clock and parlor furniture in a Steubenville court before a judge, jury, and three attorneys.

Hopelessly infatuated, Frank's ardor had culminated in an offer to marry Lulu. In court testimony, he recalled three proposals, including once when they were out riding together.

Lulu remembered only one offer of matrimony. The pair was on a walk near Reed's Mill, a pastoral spot a few miles from the Wheaton farm. Frank kept it simple. "Lulu, won't you marry me?"

Lulu testified she had answered, "No, Frank, I never will. You must not get such an idea in your head. You are too old for me, and I don't want you anyway." She elaborated to the court, "He threw out some hints afterwards which were discouraged. I told him I was going to help Mother get a set of parlor furniture."

Sniffing an opportunity, Frank dangled new bait. He would help her buy the furniture if she moved back to the farm and worked for his mother while he made a trip to Chicago.

Lulu said, "I told him if there was any idea of courtship in it, I did not want it. He said there was not."

Her mother caught wind of the deal and confronted Frank. Lizzie told the court,

"If he was trying to coax her into a marriage, she (Lulu) would have nothing to do with the furniture."

Lulu claimed, "I earned all I got."

Indeed, she did. Frank went with Lulu to buy furniture from a local man Theodore Horne. Frank told Theodore he was helping to pay for it because Lulu "was his little cousin." Frank gave Horne thirty-five dollars in cash and a check for fifteen dollars. Lulu left her watch with the businessman as a security deposit. Frank's check bounced. To recoup the fifteen dollars, Horne sold Lulu's watch for eight dollars then charged her the remaining seven dollars.

Around this time, determined to improve her mother's home, Lulu bought a mantle clock. The clock had an equestrian motif with a bronze-appearing horse on its top. The store offered an installment plan, so Lulu paid a dollar down and took the clock home. Her mother scratched together the rest of the cost over time, paying one small sum after another.

Lulu did not return to Frank's farm, so he adjusted his

scheme. The plan still depended on a journey. When the day came for Frank's trip, the ever-vigilant Lizzie noticed Lulu flitting around the house, going from here to there like a dragonfly on a summer's day. Lizzie called a halt and questioned her daughter. Lulu was going to ride the train on an outing with Frank, she explained. She'd debark at Dennison, fifty miles away, and return home. Frank would continue on to Chicago.

Lizzie didn't need to be much of a fortune teller to see where things were headed. She forbade Lulu to go. Lizzie then dealt with Frank. She told him seventeen-year-old Lulu was too young for marriage, then added that when her daughter did leave the parental nest it would be with a different sort of bird than him. Frank, who had clearly believed he was feathering his own future nest with the new parlor furniture, demanded it be surrendered to him. Lizzie and Lulu refused. Lizzie kicked Frank out of her home.

Spurned, Frank sued. He was not a generous or forgiving man. If he couldn't get the girl, he would at least get the parlor furniture. He filed a replevin suit, a well-oiled, legal tool used since the 1200s to recoup wrongfully taken or held property. The usual practice was to seize the disputed property and hold it until a determination of ownership was made.

Frank's replevin suit started off in the standard way — with a move by the court to gain control of the property and secure it until a judgment was determined. Justice Zimmerman ordered the seizure of the parlor furniture and mantle clock.

The task fell to the town constable, Samuel Spottford Clement. Born into slavery in 1861 in Virginia, at nineteen Clement decided to "go North to get rich." He sought to make "large money," and, at times, he did. He drove a grocery wagon, did janitorial work at churches, but mostly labored at construction jobs.

In 1895, Clement decided to run for the elected position of constable. His wife, Sophronia, thought this unwise. Clement dearly loved Sophronia. "There seems to be a cemented fondness between us that will last forever… Oft times she has vexed me to my very soul, until I felt like eating my own flesh and when I would turn to study the matter over, I found myself most every time in fault."

Samuel Spottford Clement, frontispiece of *Memoirs of Samuel Spottford Clement: Relating Interesting Experiences in Days of Slavery and Freedom*, by Samuel Spottford Clement, the Herald Printing Company, April 1908.

On this occasion, he ignored Sophronia's counsel. He ran against a field of five White men and won. In March 1895, Clement became the first African American elected to public office in Jefferson County's history.

As constable, Clement rubbed shoulders with judges and lawyers, murderers and bunco artists. His first arrest was of a boat-dwelling woman accused of mistreating her children. To satisfy bad debts, as ordered by the court, he gathered horses and saddles and arranged their sale. In another case, he served as auctioneer to sell a store's inventory. Clement transported prisoners on his own. This might mean a train ride to a workhouse or one to Columbus to fetch a pair of convicts in manacles.

On Monday, September 16, 1895, after Justice Zimmerman asked Clement to collect Lulu's furniture, the constable headed out with Charles Boulier in Boulier's express wagon. On the face of it, the job sounded easy: pick up furniture from some women. The men arrived at Lizzie's home by 1:30 p.m. No one answered the door. Everything was "tightly barricaded." They left and returned around four p.m. Lulu, Lizzie, and Lulu's grandmother Dorcas were home but refused entry to the men. Constable Clement attempted to pry a window open. Eighty-one-year-old Dorcas "brought a cane down on his hand with more force than was pleasant."

Changing tactics, but not strategy, Clement broke open the front door. Dorcas stuck with her dedication to violence. She struck him over the head and nose with her cane.

Dogged in his determination, the constable grabbed the mantle clock at which point Lizzie jumped into the fray. She lit into him. In the scuffle, the clock fell to the ground. The fake-bronze horse revealed its true, breakable nature and shattered. Boulier attempted to restrain Dorcas. The octogenarian rewarded the man with a chair over his head and treated him to language "more forcible than elegant."

After considerable resistance, the furniture was loaded up and carried away. However, a chair had been overlooked. The two battered men returned. A sniffling Lulu showed the constable upstairs and the chair was removed without incident.

Constable Clement filed an affidavit for assault and battery and resisting an officer against Lizzie and Dorcas. Making a third trip to Adams Street that evening, he was greeted by a large crowd. The three women were not home.

On Tuesday, September 17th, Lizzie Parr appeared, pled guilty to Clement's charges, and was fined twenty dollars and costs. Lulu tearfully pled for leniency with her mother. She said fifteen dollars was all the money they had. The tears worked. The judge settled for that sum. Dorcas was not fined due to her age.

Friday, September 20th, was spent in court with three lawyers — "Messrs. McCauslen, Taylor, and Rogers" — handling the attempt to retrieve the furniture and clock with a jury trial. Lulu and Lizzie detailed their dealings with Frank Wheaton. Frank, on his part, ungallantly claimed to have hugged and kissed Lulu "at least four thousand times." His churlish comment zinged along American telegraph lines to be printed as a gossipy tidbit from coast to coast. Four thousand kisses were more than enough to titillate the Victorian-age readers.

Lulu denied any courting with Frank Wheaton. She testified she'd never kept company nor sat up at night nor stayed with him alone. The teenager underlined her testimony with an angry outburst that Frank's claim of intimacy was false "And you [Frank] know it is."

Lulu then detailed Frank's fiscal shenanigans. Other

witnesses claimed Lulu wanted Frank to invest two hundred dollars in show business.

The jury returned a verdict after forty minutes. Lulu could keep the furniture.

Thanks to the newly formed AP wire service, thousands of Americans were privy then and in later years to Frank Wheaton's picadilloes with women and horses. Though Frank shared Lulu's interest in equines, he may not have been the most compassionate horseman. In 1896, he was arrested and fined five dollars for leaving his horse out in the July heat all day without water or food. He made the papers again in 1906 when his purchase of a new horse was announced with his claim that he thought he "had a flyer," a speedy one, in the piece of horseflesh.

After the replevin case with Lulu, Frank would not talk a woman into marrying him for another eight years. His bride left him less than a year later. Frank took her to court, seeking a stay. He claimed that one day after they had separated, while he was at work on the railroad, she and her sister went to his house and removed clothing and household goods. Frank said if his wife wanted to be in the house or have any goods, she should return to their marital home. He succeeded in gaining a restraining order. The couple reconciled and went on to raise a family of four children.

For Lulu, the press coverage of her fight with her cousin marked the beginning of her public life. Americans might chortle over their morning coffee as they read the details of her teenage love life. They might laugh out loud to read that not one of the three women could state the year of their birth. They might even snicker over the report that Lulu's mother earned her living as a fortune teller. But they learned a name to remember: Lulu Parr.

DORCAS'S ORIGIN STORY

North Fork of the Little Beaver Creek, Beaver County, Pennsylvania
1813

Constable Clement and Mr. Boulier should not have been surprised by Dorcas Myers' feistiness. Lulu's grandmother Dorcas was born June 21, 1813, and raised in a not-quite-mainstream situation. She grew up across the Ohio River in Beaver County, Pennsylvania, one of a dozen or so children born to George and Catherine Foulks. George built a two-story, sturdy sandstone home for his family. According to one account, the property was "littered with wigwams and rickety cabins" housing Native Americans. George ran a trading post out of his home. The Native Americans trusted George and appreciated his ability to converse in six Native American dialects.

George was also well thought of by Whites. He stood five feet and ten inches and weighed about one hundred and seventy-five pounds and was a "very fine looking man." More importantly, he was "… a man of first-rate character, remarkably kind to his family." Another writer noted, "He was a man that was respected by all who knew him, a worthy husband and a kind and affectionate father, at an early part of his life he became a member of the Presbyterian Church to which he remained up to his death."

George's linguistic skills and ease with Native American culture was rooted in a life-shattering, well-publicized event. Though the precise details vary, the majority of recountings agree on the major points.

George Foulks was born in Leesburg, Virginia on December 4, 1769. Originally from Pennsylvania, the family lived in Leesburg for several years. His father, a carpenter, purchased land beside the courthouse and attempted to make money by building houses "on spec." His flips flopped. "His expenses apparently surpassed his progress and Foulks was forced to sell at a loss," is how he would be remembered in Virginia. The Foulks family, impoverished by their real estate business failure, moved to Pennsylvania. They settled west of Pittsburgh in what would become Beaver County. When George was ten years old, his father dropped dead at the plow. His mother remarried.

In March of 1780, after a particularly cold winter, eleven-year-old George set off on an adventure. He, along with his twenty-one-year-old brother John, sixteen-year-old sister Elizabeth, his stepsiblings, and neighbors headed to Raccoon Creek. His mother stayed behind with the younger children.

It was late winter — or, in the eyes of the optimistic, very early spring. Sweet clear sap was rising in the sugar maple trees. The young people would spend days tapping the maples, and collecting, straining, and boiling down the sap to make syrup and maple sugar. The work was not difficult, but it did take time as over forty gallons of sap were needed for each gallon of maple syrup. Sugaring off was a joyful break for the frontier children.

A Sugar Camp. Illustration from *The Big Sandy Valley: A History of the People and Country from the Earliest Settlement to the Present Time.* 1887. Courtesy Library of Congress.

By Monday, March 20th, the sugar camp was eight to ten days into their endeavor. The young men and boys did some target shooting in the afternoon. On a hill 300 yards away, six or so Wyandottes spied on them. When dusk fell, the youngsters trailed off to hunt raccoons.

The Wyandottes hunkered down in the brush, silent. With the patience of all successful predators, the men bided their time. Their mission was to steal human prey, not syrup. The raid, what the Iroquois called a "mourning war," would replenish their depleted tribe.

The tactic, followed by multiple Native American tribes from New England to Texas hill country, was intended to ease the losses from warfare and disease — to keep the tribe strong and well-manned. Small raiding bands typically traveled one hundred, two hundred, or more miles from their home to locate quarry. Distance was their ally. It created an element of surprise and obscured the location of their homeland.

Though some captives were tortured and killed, often children were abducted for adoption into the tribe. Preferentially, the children were latent age, from around six to twelve or so — a developmental stage marked by pliability and educability. Their fresh minds were absorbent, ripe for learning new ways. Old enough to avoid all the fuss consumed by infants and toddlers, they had not yet mutated into the riotous, prickly beings of full-force adolescents.

The Wyandotte tribe, also known as the Hurons, sorely needed additional manpower. Originally from north of Lake Ontario, they had allied with the French. The outcome was disastrous. Lethal conflict with the Iroquois and their British allies cost the Wyandottes many lives. Diseases of European origin swept away up to half their population. By the 1700s, the Wyandottes had shrunk from an estimated 40,000 tribal members before European contact to 12,000 survivors living in northwest Ohio.

The raid on the Raccoon Creek sugar camp was the first

of a 1780 spate of attacks on the settlers who had dared to make homes in the region west of Pittsburgh.

Oblivious to the Wyandottes' presence, George, his brother John, and the other raccoon hunters returned to camp around eleven. Later, some would recall the dogs as fussing and barking.

Four of the young men bunked down in a lean-to. The six children lay before them, closer to the fire. George's brother John crawled with his rifle and white dog, Ginger, into one of the large wooden troughs to rest. George's sister Elizabeth decided to brew a spring tonic, sassafras tea, and needed a sweetener. She sent George out to get the sap from one of the tapped trees.

Midnight. The full moon shone at its brightest. Like a giant astronomical mirror, its reflected light illuminated George's world and ended a journey of ninety-three million miles from the sun to fizzle out in the grove of sugar maples. George trudged on through the dead, rustling leaves. Even though April was coming soon, the night was frosty. There was no snow on the ground.

George picked a tree.

The wrong one.

George Foulk's world exploded.

One of the Wyandottes leapt from behind the maple, struck George in the head with the pipe end of his tomahawk, and knocked the boy unconscious.

When George roused himself to consciousness, he was captive, a string around his neck, and seated before the fire pit.

The melee was on. The White youths, rather than fight, fled. John Foulks' white dog, Ginger, ran with him, became tangled in his feet, and tripped him. The Wyandottes tomahawked John to death and scalped him. Four other

Whites died at the hands of the Wyandotte band.

Six children were now in the hands of a band of nine warring Wyandottes. They were from the village of Junquindundeh. Three of the captors were sons of the village's chief, Half King, also known as Dunquat or Pamoacan. The abducted children included George, his sister Elizabeth, their two stepsiblings, and two neighbor children. There is no claim, no oral history, and no record of anyone escaping the ambush except those kidnapped by the Wyandottes.

The men hustled their human bounty along. They had left horses waiting by the banks of the Ohio River, enough for all the girls to ride. Before they were mounted on the horses, the girls' gowns were cut off to ease travel, their shoes tossed into the Ohio River. The Wyandottes had come prepared, bringing moccasins with them which they slipped on the children's feet. The transformation of the children into Wyandottes had begun.

Huron [Wyandotte] moccasins. Circa 1880. Exhibit in Bata Shoe Museum, Toronto, Ontario, Canada.

Hurrying like foxes with chickens in their jaws, the Wyandottes sped from the White world and headed home. Their destination lay in western Ohio, nearly two hundred miles away. Located on the Sandusky River, Whites would rename it Fremont in 1859. There was no time taken to cook. Food was limited to scraps of dried venison.

There was also no time taken to care for George's head wound. Weak from blood loss, the boy walked. Elizabeth would put him on her pony, but the Wyandottes repeatedly pulled him off. The youngsters had spunk. Elizabeth tore bits of her clothing and dropped them along the trail to help her family find her. But no one was looking for her. The lack of snow made tracking impossible, and the settlers launched no recovery effort. The five dead young men at the sugar camp were buried in a mass grave.

At one point, one of the Wyandottes knocked George off a log they were walking on to bridge a creek. George fell in the water and calmly crawled out and continued on. When the opportunity arose, George returned the favor and tripped the fellow into the water. This seemed to gain him favor at least with the other captors, if not his drenched victim.

High water at the Tuscarawas River did not stop the group, though they had no canoe. The Wyandottes fastened the children to a sapling to keep their heads above water, placed it in the river and swam alongside as they pushed the children across.

The fleeing band took no respite until they had traveled over one hundred miles. At a Native American settlement known as Old Town or Snip's Town, they finally stopped. They had their first hot meal — hominy, venison, and wild turkey boiled in maple sugar water. George's wound was dressed with slippery elm bark and bear's oil. As they were children, they did not have to run the gauntlet as adult captives typically did.

A hundred more miles on foot and horseback and the group reached Junquindundeh. There, on the banks of the lower Sandusky River, the captives were divvied up like game after a hunt. George was given to a family with an experienced mother, one who had raised several children. Elizabeth became the child of one of Half King's sons.

Three days after their arrival, the village held a feast in honor of the captives, their new family members. Young George was stripped naked, taken out into the Sandusky River, and scrubbed by several Native American women with river pebbles in a ritual adoption. All the children would be treated as well, or at least no worse, than other Wyandotte youth.

George and Elizabeth learned their brother John's fate when they recognized his curly, black-haired scalp as it was being dressed. With the American Revolutionary War in full throttle, scalping had become a military tool. Patriots and British alike were accused of buying enemy scalps from their Native American allies. John's scalp may have been destined for a bounty sale to the Wyandottes' British allies. Later, the Wyandottes would tell George that, if not for the white dog, John would have escaped.

The two Foulks' spinning world skewed, rotated, and with an immutable shift, transported them to a different reality. Their tongues became adept at rolling out Wyandotte syllables, words, and sentences. Their eyes saw Wyandotte ways to approach and solve problems. For instance, when smallpox broke out in the village, George's adoptive father took protective action. He brought two live skunks into their living quarters. Each day he would annoy them with a switch from a bush, tapping them, and driving them about until they let loose with their best defense. The aroma shielded the family from smallpox by discouraging outside visitors.

Life with the Wyandottes changed George and Elizabeth's minds. While Whites would later wistfully dream the two remained White inside while outwardly adopting Wyandotte ways, that was not the case. The two Foulks assimilated and would thereafter remain a blend of both worlds, the Wyandotte and the White. Coming to manhood with a people whose men hunted and warred and only women raised crops, George would find the plow boring.

Life with the Wyandottes forged an invisible, yet powerful bond. Like others captured and adopted as children, he became enculturated into his new culture and would never fully abandon it.

In the fall of 1786, George made a journey back east and visited his mother. He was sixteen, old enough to be considered a man. Quite likely his adopted family was confident in the strength of his ties to the Wyandotte world. They were correct. He returned to Junquindundeh. George lived with the Wyandotte for a decade. He said he never took part in any of the Wyandotte's expeditions against the Whites, though this may have been a face-saving statement. He followed custom in his marriage with a Wyandotte woman. She bore him two children.

Eventually George decided to return to White society. The Wyandottes were allied with the British and George most likely did not want to end up on the wrong side of any coming conflict between the United States and Great Britain. Pressure was building to oust the Native Americans from northern Ohio. It was time, in George's assessment, to go.

He began staying out for longer and longer periods of time to hunt. He cached food on his planned escape route. He

I Ain't Afraid

had his own horses. Finally, one day, he announced he would be hunting in a place west of the village and rode west, but then circled until he was headed east. He rode his horse and when the horse died, he walked the remaining one hundred and twenty-some miles. Finally, he was at the banks of the Ohio River near present-day Sewickley in Allegheny County, Pennsylvania. The trip had taken thirteen days. Across the river was the Ullerys' family cabin. Though he was dressed as a Wyandotte, one or two of the Ullery girls rowed over and carried him to the south bank.

His parents had never abandoned the homesite east of Pittsburgh.

George, coming from the Wyandotte culture in which only women raised crops, disdained farming. He became a spy against the Native Americans in the Indian War of 1790, serving the United States government under Samuel Brady. For four years, he tapped into his knowledge of Native American languages and culture, traveling up and down the Ohio River corridor.

While in the service of Captain Samuel Brady, George was hired by a Mr. Casselman. Two of Casselman's daughters had, like George, been abducted by the Wyandottes. Mr. Casselman paid George to steal his children back from the Wyandots. George succeeded in taking Molly and Polly Casselman from their captors. The Wyandottes trailed them but were unable to overtake them. One of the girls had married an Indian while in captivity and had given birth to a daughter. She later married a White man.

George's work as a spy ended when General "Mad" Anthony Wayne made his advance to the west and was victorious over allied Native Americans and British forces in the 1794 Battle of Fallen Timbers. For his service, George received a grant of land. He married Catherine, one of the Ullery girls, and settled on his land on Little Beaver Creek in Beaver County, Pennsylvania. Although he had taken a Wyandotte woman as his partner, it is unlikely he felt any necessity to seek a divorce from her as their union would not have been legally recognized in the White world.

George built a mill on the creek and supplemented his income through trade with the Native Americans. His home served as a trading post and his land was described as "cluttered with wigwams and rickety cabins built by Indians who trusted George." Twice yearly, he went to Pittsburgh to buy trade goods. At times, he traveled back to Junquindundeh to trade calico, trinkets, traps, jewelry, and liquor for furs. His adoptive Native American mother helped him as he bartered and traded with the Wyandottes.

Elizabeth, George's sister, made Junquindundeh and her nearby property her life-long home after her abduction at sixteen. She developed a relationship with a fellow White captive, James Whitacre. They married and spent their lives in and near the village, running a trading post on over one thousand acres gifted to them by the Wyandottes. Theirs was considered to be the first continuously occupied home by a White family in Ohio. At least once, Elizabeth traveled back to Pennsylvania with her infant on the saddle in front of her. Accompanied by two Wyandotte women, she visited with her mother and family, showed off her baby, then rode back to Ohio with her child and Wyandotte companions.

George bought land in Richland County, Ohio, an area he came to know first as an abducted eleven-year-old on his trek to Junquindundeh. He never lived in Richland, but at least six of his children settled there, including Dorcas. She moved there after her father George's death, and it was there she married George H. Myers in 1844.

George's ties with the Wyandottes would reverberate down through the coming generations. His Wyandotte heritage colored and shaped his descendants' choices, actions, and pleasures. Nowhere would the persisting patterns of his Indigenous world be more evident than in the life of his great-granddaughter Lulu Bell Parr.

MARRYING TIME

Steubenville, Ohio
1896

For Dorcas's granddaughter Lulu, the path forward must have looked narrow and the horizon low at age nineteen. Keeping her life well within the constraints of tradition, she married George Barrett on March 31, 1896. A Justice of the Peace performed the ceremony.

George Washington Barrett, twenty-three years old, was Steubenville born and raised. He came from a family of six children. Their father, a Civil War veteran, worked various jobs including blacksmithing and laboring at a blast furnace. George, too, earned his way with his hands, often with the steam-powered industrial machines of the time. A few months after his marriage to Lulu, George was hired on as the fireman for the new Steubenville water works.

Lulu's brother William married Glendora "Dora" Dohrmer on December 21, 1898. She was a young widow, only twenty-three years old. Eleven months earlier her prior husband had died of typhoid less than two months after their marriage. William was Dora's third husband. Initially, William and Dora shared the family duplex on Adams Street with Lulu and George. They then hopscotched from rental to rental in the Steubenville area. William worked for the railroad.

Lulu would also move around. In early June 1900, four years into their marriage, the Census taker found the Barretts living in a rented house at 503 Sinclair Avenue in Steubenville. Ribbonlike, their street wound through the outskirts of town. Brush-and-tree-covered hills crowded it. Like a bracelet missing many of its charms, modest homes lay strung along the road. Sinclair was one of those lonely, poverty-infused side roads common in the Appalachians — the kind of place where sadness and violence thrum below the surface. George worked with boilers — a hot, hard, sweaty job. Lulu remained at home. According to the Census Report, she had not birthed any children.

Other working-class families lived in the area — potters, railroad workers, laborers, a stone mason, and a jewelry polisher. One of them was the Sanders family with their six children. Capitola Sanders' husband was out of town when the Census taker came round and was still away on June 5. Capitola left her children that day to do housework uptown, most likely as a maid. In the afternoon, Lulu was out and about when she discovered the body of Capitola's youngest, two-and-a-half-year-old Willie. He'd wandered out onto the railroad tracks and been struck by a westbound Panhandle train, his body crushed and cut in half. Lulu immediately ran to the neighbors for help. The *Steubenville Herald-Star* reported the death and Lulu's part in the story. The town mourned the little boy.

Lulu's name did not appear again in the local paper until the next year.

The *Steubenville Herald* on August 16, 1901, listed among the court reports was this notice:

Diane Helentjaris

Lula Barrett vs George Barrett for divorce. They were married Jan. [sic] 31, 1896, and she alleges that on July 15, 1901, defendant placed a loaded revolver at plaintiff's breast and threatened her life and choked her and otherwise abused her.

Whether it was the gun, the verbal threat, or the strangulation, Lulu recognized her risk. She extricated herself from the disastrous situation. The two separated. By 1902, they were living apart. Listed as "Mrs. Lulu Barrett," Lulu roomed at 123 South Fourth Street. George Barrett, worked as a boilermaker and boarded at 232 South Fourth Street, only a block from Lulu. Their divorce case, scheduled for May 5, 1902, was granted on the grounds of extreme cruelty.

Steubenville, O. South Fourth St. Postcard. Author's collection.

I Ain't Afraid

George moved on romantically. He remarried, raised four children with his second wife, and after her death, took a third wife. He continued to make his living as a skilled laborer and never left Steubenville.

Lulu roomed above the Buckeye Waterproof Sign Company. Proprietor and printer Benjamin F. Hipsley lived and worked at the address with his wife, Maud. Maud was a few months older than Lulu and from nearby Columbiana County. Her husband was twelve years older than the two women. A crusty man, he had served time in a Pennsylvania county workhouse for disorderly conduct but had not learned his lesson. He was in hot water again in 1899, this time in Steubenville's Mayor's Court for profanity and, again, disorderly conduct.

Lulu found herself in the socially denigrated position afforded divorced women at the time. Not everyone listed as a widow in the City Directories of America had a dead husband. Some, including Lulu, were "grass widows." They were women whose husbands had passed on in a sense, but were still above ground, in the grass, walking around, and enjoying life.

The expectations for a young woman in Lulu's circumstances were low, very low.

METAMORPHOSIS

Bloomington, Illinois
1860

Unlike Lulu's diminished expectations and cramped horizon, her future mentor Gordon William Lillie's skyline was vast. Wide open skies, miles of nothingness, sparse settlements, looseness of law. The American West, like negative space in a painting, offers a blank canvas ripe for innovation, creativity, and even…resurrection. Men, women, and families head West, peel off their identities like Monarch butterflies shedding their cocoons, to emerge as new, reinvented beings.

Gordon William Lillie and May Manning succeeded in such a transformation. No one could have predicted the trajectory of their lives. Born in 1860 in Bloomington, Illinois, Gordon William Lillie was a city boy. Hometown folks would remember him as a pudgy-faced, "sissified," and frail child, more at ease playing with girls than rough-housing. He claimed to have, at a butcher's suggestion, improved his health by drinking still-warm blood from slaughtered animals. Bookish, Lillie graduated high school in 1879 and briefly taught school.

By 1880, Gordon, his parents, brother, and two sisters

immigrated to Wellington, Kansas. Gordon's sister Effie would later recall, "…we came in a covered wagon. My uncle was a carpenter, so he built us a one-room home on the claim with a dirt floor. It was a very meager home, not at all what we had been used to. We cooked, ate, and slept in the same room."

The Lillies weren't the only ones on the move. The Pawnee tribe was headed south through Kansas, on their way to Indian Territory. Like an inexorable wind blowing from east to west, the United States government's policy of "Indian removal" swept Native Americans from their ancestral homes. Treaties, wars, infectious disease, shady deals, and annihilation shoved them along. Their destination was Indian Territory, a misnomer of epic proportion. These new lands to which the Native Americans ran, rode, fled, and walked were already peopled by other tribes. This led, in a cascade of falling dominos, to warring between the Native American tribes. Indian Territory was an ephemeral concept, only lasting as long as the Territory stayed free of White land lust. Eventually, each Indian Territory shrank and disappeared under the pressure of White immigration and resource exploitation.

Pawnee Indians, 1861/1869 by George Catlin. Courtesy of National Gallery of Art.

For the Pawnee tribe, their ancestral home was centered in Nebraska and Kansas. In their heyday, they led a semi-nomadic life on the rolling plains. They gathered fruit, berries, nuts, and roots from the wild. The women raised ten varieties of corn and eight of beans along with melons, squash, pumpkins, and sunflowers. The Pawnees' domed earthen lodges, each home to as many as forty people, overlooked the rivers like clusters of giant beehives. Wisps of smoke from cook fires lazily trailed from the single eye-like openings which pierced the top of each lodge. An entrance faced the east and inside, a horned buffalo skull welcomed people. In sync with the changing seasons, they'd temporarily leave their villages of lodges to wage war or hunt game, sleeping in teepees. The men hunted bison and antelope.

Pawnee Indian lodge. Circa 1908. Lulu had a copy of this image in her personal collection. Courtesy of Library of Congress.

Infectious diseases, crop failures, and warfare with encroaching tribes — especially the Sioux — decimated the Pawnees. By the 1870s, only 2,400 members remained of a tribe once boasting ten to sixty-thousand members. With few options, the Pawnees sold their Nebraska land holdings and bought 283,000 acres in the remaining pot-shaped piece of geography, south of Kansas, deemed Indian Territory.

Within a few years, the government would open large swaths of it to White settlement. It would become the state of Oklahoma. The Pawnees' land would give rise to Pawnee County, Oklahoma.

No longer would the Pawnees roam the grasslands. Food would be doled out at the Commissary on Saturdays to the Pawnees, "…coffee, beans, potatoes, and the like." No longer would their children sleep under the loving eyes of their kin. Instead, their beds were cots in a sparsely staffed dormitory at a boarding school in the town bearing their tribe's name.

Catching Wild Horses – Pawnee, 1861/1869 by George Catlin.
Courtesy of National Gallery of Art.

I Ain't Afraid

A White Indian Agent was assigned to oversee the Pawnees. As if the United States feared losing the upper hand in the ongoing land grabs, government buildings went up quickly. Blocks of tan to red local sandstone were cut and mortared into a twenty-by-forty-foot Indian Agent office and a two-story boarding school dormitory. In the rush, the cement for the dormitory well wasn't properly cured, delaying the opening until the fall of 1878. Dubbed the Pawnee Industrial School, its purpose was to assimilate, to transform the Pawnees into farmers by training and educating their children. The cluster of government buildings gave rise to the county seat, also known as Pawnee.

The Lillie family's fate intertwined with that of the Pawnee tribe. In a July 1881 government report on the Indian Agencies, Gordon's father was listed as a baker and his mother, a cook at the Pawnee Agency for respective salaries of 300 and 400 dollars.

Effie Lillie explained,

> *My brother Gordon was teaching at the Pawnee Agency and got the job of steward and stewardess for my father and mother...*
>
> *At first, we went to school with the Indian children... There were from a hundred to two hundred children enrolled. The children were from six years old until some were grown in size. They were detailed to do the work, and, in that way, they learned to work as well as to talk English and to get a book education. There was a seamstress whose duty was to over-see the girls in the sewing room. The matron and assistant matron taught them and looked over the dining-room manners. There*

was a playroom for the rainy days but on pretty days they played outside at recess. All of them slept in a big dormitory and they had to make their own beds in the morning when they got up. There was an Indian truant officer who went and got any child who ran away and brought it back… The boys were detailed to mix the bread which was made in big tubs. Sixty loaves were baked two or three times a week. Mother and father both oversaw the bread making. The girls would put it in the pans. Father would build a fire in the great big rock ovens and when it was right, he would rake the coals out and the rocks would be hot enough to bake the bread evenly. He knew just how much fire to use to bake it…

When Gordon was teaching at Pawnee, he learned the Indian language. A man from Buffalo Bill Cody's show came to the Agency to get Indians to play in his show. Gordon went with them as an interpreter.

If moving west was pivotal for Gordon Lillie, connecting with Buffalo Bill Cody locked the compass of his life as would happen years later when Lulu crossed Cody's pathway. Buffalo Bill's Wild West was a new show when Lillie was hired in 1883. It would become the most popular form of American entertainment for decades.

Few could match the level of adventure and excitement in founder William F "Buffalo Bill" Cody's origin story. As a fifteen-year-old whippersnapper, he claimed to have carried mail for the Pony Express. He served in the Union Army during the Civil War. As a scout for the Army in the Indian

Wars, he received the Congressional Medal of Honor. The tall handsome man dipped a toe in theatrics, then ventured off to develop the quintessential Wild West Show.

Seated on a white horse, his mustache dripping into his goatee, he would ride up and majestically doff his wide-brimmed Stetson to the audience. Kids yelled, men were thrilled, and women – well, women loved him, and he loved them back, much to his wife's chagrin. Cody was one of those broad-minded individuals who took others at face value.

Thirteen years Lillie's senior, Buffalo Bill became his mentor, professional colleague, sometimes partner, and — for most of the time — his friend. Gordon William Lillie began to dress in fringed buckskin, a colorful scarf about his neck, a slouchy hat atop his head, boots on his feet. He became Pawnee Bill and somewhere along the way picked up rank as Major Gordon W. Lillie. Mythmakers were enlisted to pad his life experience with adventures among the Native Americans, the buffalo, cowboys, and crooks. The chubby, weak, and sedentary boy grew up to be a Man of the West.

Major Gordon W. Lillie, "Pawnee Bill." Postcard. Author's collection.

Like a theme circus, Buffalo Bill's Wild West followed a tried-and-true format. The whole shebang – horses, camels, tents, bandwagons, and performers — rumbled across the country by railroad from spring to autumn. Most shows were in the east. An advance team traveled ahead to make arrangements, buy food, scout pasturage along town creeks for the American bison, set up open-air arenas, and distribute colorful handbills and posters. Newspapers —small town little papers and big city editions — breathlessly published photos, schedules, and gossipy articles about the Wild West show alongside advertisements.

The public was encouraged to mill about while the show was being set up, to wander around the Native Americans' teepees and to interact with the staff. The Wild West Show set things off in a town with a free parade. Buffalo Bill on his white horse, cowboy bands blaring rhythmic music, pretty cowgirls, colorful ornate wagons, and Native Americans traipsed through town and quickened bystanders' hearts. Not only an enticement to buy tickets to the show, the parade was also an intentional gift of free entertainment to the poor. An afternoon matinee and an evening show followed the opening parade. Sunday was a day off.

The shows touted themselves as educational, peopled by genuine cowboys and cowgirls, folks raised on the plains, and expert in ranching skills. Native American performers were a critical part of the cast. Those well-known Native Americans who had once waged war on the Whites, who fought at the Little Big Horn, chiefs such as Sitting Bull and renegades like Geronimo were highly prized. Americans thrilled to see these former foes upfront and personal.

W.F. Cody "Buffalo Bill" shooting glass ball targets with Lakota man at his side. 1907. Courtesy of Library of Congress.

On June 7, 1886, Pawnee Bill rode out in Buffalo Bill's Wild West opening parade. This parade was scheduled to reach Broad and Chestnut Street in downtown Philadelphia by ten-thirty in the morning. Somewhere along the parade route, the twenty-four-year-old met his kismet. Pawnee Bill was gobsmacked by a laughing teenager, a Smith College Quaker girl, standing on the sidewalk. Big-eyed, wide-mouthed, with luxuriant dark wavy hair and a sturdy build, she captured his heart.

May Manning hardly fit the stereotype of a born-on-the-farm pioneer woman. Her father had earned his living, according to the 1870 census, as a blacksmith with a personal estate worth one hundred dollars. It was the lowest amount census enumerators were permitted to document. Maybe the poverty of forging horseshoes spurred him on or maybe the inherent properties of metal intrigued him. Whatever the case, ten years later, May's father had transformed himself into a "magnetic physician" and even later, an "electric physician."

The potential therapeutic powers of electricity and magnetism captivated scientists, charlatans, and the general public alike in the 19th century. Advances such as electrocardiograms and electrocautery of wounds became a routine part of American medicine. Other, unproven, treatments such as electric brushes to treat baldness, were sold direct to consumers. Among the most popular quackery were electropathic belts. These contraptions of wires, copper, and silver-coated zinc zapped wearers with small jolts of electricity. Advertisements claimed success in treating impotence, hernias, exhaustion, liver disease, unsatisfactory sexual performance, and more. Electric and magnetic medicine was a rich career field to plow in the 1800s.

Despite his own eccentric background, May Manning's father expected a more straitlaced suitor for his fifteen-year-old daughter than a fellow who called himself "Pawnee

Bill." But the heart has a way. Pawnee Bill was determined to win her. Letters flew across the continent, back and forth, between the two. The pair courted for two years then married. May would claim to be eighteen on the marriage certificate, though she may have been a year or so younger.

Their marriage was the antithesis of Buffalo Bill and his wife Louisa's. The Cody union was marked by Bill's infidelity, his claims that Louisa attempted to poison him, an abortive divorce filing, and discord among their children.

In contrast, Pawnee Bill and May were deeply devoted to each other. May gave birth to their first child, a son, who died soon after. Unable to have another child, she threw herself into becoming a Wild West cowgirl. She learned to shoot and ride and, billed as the "Champion Girl Horseback Shot of the West," starred in the couple's own Pawnee Bill's Wild West Show.

Pawnee Bill and May Lillie's show became the second-best-known Wild West show in America, only surpassed by Cody. All they needed to do for their success was to mimic Cody, but without the poor business skills dogging the charismatic showman.

The Great Pawnee Bill Shows The Only Genuine Wild West. Circa 1903. Poster. Courtesy of Library of Congress.

By spring of 1903, Pawnee Bill's Wild West show was popular and financially successful, though it trailed behind Buffalo Bill Cody's show in cachet. Pawnee Bill owned an

8,000-acre ranch in Oklahoma where he kept the largest bison herd in the country. As befitting the president of the local bank, his signature graced five-dollar bank notes. To the consternation of competitors, he insisted on appending "Pawnee Bill" at the end of his signature on each note. They hollered "unfair" and "undue advertising."

Pawnee Bill and May had strategically located the show's winter headquarters in Carnegie, a suburb of Pittsburgh. Close to the population centers on the East Coast and the Midwest, the location saved transportation costs.

The prior autumn, things had gone about as well as could be expected. In October, while moving forty-eight ponies from winter headquarters to a nearby town, nine had made a break for freedom. Three hours later they were caught and back where they should be.

Later that month, a group of the show's Native American performers made news as they traveled home for the winter. Minnie Strong, wife of Milton Strong, gave birth to their baby on the Pennsylvania and Vandalia Railroad train somewhere between Terre Haute, Indiana and Effingham, Illinois. As the train neared St. Louis where they were to switch to the Wabash Railroad, the Native Americans began to paint their faces. When the train stopped at Union Station, the group poured off the train and began to sing and dance, setting off a cultural misunderstanding. Frightened Whites called the police. After half an hour, the police convinced the Native Americans to stop. They were then "safely locked away" on the train awaiting the next leg of their journey. A leader of the Native Americans explained the singing and dancing was a ceremony designed to protect the baby, especially given its non-traditional birth site. The child was reportedly named "Forty Miles An Hour." The Native Americans had squeezed in a blessing ceremony before reaching the constraints of the reservation where traditional dances and ceremonies were outlawed.

Over the winter, Pawnee Bill had brought fifty Filipinos to his winter headquarters at Carnegie. They were seasoned fighters, veterans of the recent Philippine-American war, an outgrowth of the better-known Spanish-American War.

Now it was spring. The Filipinos joined with Russian Cossacks, cowboys, cowgirls, Japanese acrobats, Arabian tumblers, and thirty Native Americans with their wives and children in Carnegie in anticipation of the new season. At least twenty-two languages were spoken by the performers and workers. All told, about 500 people would tour along with 400 horses, fifty ponies, a dozen bison (including a revered white buffalo), and twenty burros. The performers, livestock, hand-carved show wagons, tents, lights, saddles, canvas, and other paraphernalia filled twenty to thirty railcars. The logistics of moving Wild West shows from place to place, of quickly and safely loading animals, supplies, and people, would be used later as a model for military tactics.

The 1903 Show was named "Pawnee Bill's Historic Wild West Show." After a kickoff May 6 in Pittsburgh, the show chugged west to bring the thrills of the Old West to rural Ohio.

Gordon W. Lillie, "Pawnee Bill." Circa 1890. Courtesy Denver Public Library Digital Collections.

Meanwhile, in Steubenville, life went on for the divorced

I Ain't Afraid

Lulu. The Hipsley family still lived over the Buckeye Waterproof Sign Company. Mrs. Hipsley — Maud — gave birth April 7 to their son, Benjamin. Whether Lulu (now known as Lulu Barrett) had moved out of the Hipsley home before the birth or after, whether she helped her friend care for the newborn, heard his mewling cries, or was living elsewhere is unknown. One thing is certain: in less than a week, Lulu Bell Parr Barrett would leave Steubenville.

If Lulu read the *Steubenville Herald* on Tuesday, May 8, she might have been intrigued by one advertisement in particular. It was for the Pawnee Bill Wild West Show and assured the readers that "never before were finer pictures of American manhood presented in a Wild West arena — genuine sons of the plains, with muscles of steel and hard as the sinews of a stage; Indians of many tribes, from the most venerable chiefs to the strapped papoose, exemplifying the fantastic ceremonies, strange customs, legends and barbarous torture dances…"

The Wild West Show would be in Steubenville in a week. Delayed by a trainwreck on the 14th, the afternoon show in Wheeling was canceled and the morning parade not held until seven p.m. After the evening show, everyone packed up and headed north to Steubenville, pulling in at eight in the morning.

A few years earlier, in the infamous replevins court case with her jilted suitor, there were hints of what would come to pass. Lulu's kissin' cousin Frank Wheaton had mentioned she had wanted him to invest 200 dollars so she could "perform." The type of performance had been left to the imagination. Now those who had giggled over the teenage Lulu's romantic troubles would witness the fulfillment of her dream.

Although celebrities and Native Americans worked for

Pawnee Bill under a contract, other laborers, dazzled by adventure, were drawn to the show like iron shavings to a magnet. Star-struck teenage boys might hang around the animals and make themselves useful, fetching water and such, and end up with a job. Lulu certainly knew how to ride and seemed smitten by horses. How she came to be hired by Pawnee Bill is uncertain, but somehow, she wrangled herself a spot in the show

For now, in May 1903, the twenty-six-year-old was off on a great adventure. Ahead lay Coshocton, Ohio, with folks of all ages looking forward to the June 11 parade and performances. "An army of cowboys and frontier heroes. Military reviews by detachments of the armies of the world, boomerang throwers from Australia, Hindoos and Japanese" were joined by a petite young woman who loved horses. If the past is the best prediction of the future, no one would have predicted what lay over the horizon for Lulu Bell Parr.

Except maybe Lulu.

ON THE ROAD

Northeastern Ohio
June 1903

Despite its grim danger, there is no more fascinating pastime in the field of athletic endeavor than riding "bucking" bronchos. I do it twice every day except Sunday, and it has converted me from a weak muscled, indecisive young woman to a very self-reliant and vigorous person. Let any normally healthy young woman screw up her courage, try it a few times and then mark the increased joy of living that has come.
—Lulu B. Parr, *The Santa Fe New Mexican*, 20 September 1907, Friday, page 15.

No one could blame Lulu if she were intoxicated with life. Her dream of performing had roused itself and stepped out of the shadows into daylight. She worked for Pawnee Bill now. Best of all, she had grabbed her goal without owing a thing to Frank Wheaton or his ilk. She did it on her own. Whatever her fortune-telling mother predicted, one way or another, Lulu was headed into brand-spanking new opportunities.

At twenty-six, Lulu knew she was beautiful. Described

as blonde, "a tiny bit of a young woman whose appearance does not in any way suggest the rough life of the ranch," her features were pleasingly symmetrical, her jawline well-defined. Her disarmingly feminine appearance opened doors as well as sugar-coated her strength. In a few days, when she trotted out on a fancy horse into the roped-off arena, even if she were one rider among many, she'd get more than her share of attention. She would have the eyes of the world on her, and she would show them what she could do.

The Wild West train skimmed over the steel rails, barreled through the flatness of northern Ohio. On the other side of Lulu's window, rich rolling farmland spooled out in a green ribbon. The longest day of the year, the summer solstice, beckoned ahead. June's sweet airiness and the fecund terrain charmed the roughneck Wild Westers.

The maniacal busyness of spring planting had eased for the farmers. Their crops were planted, the lambs born. The first fresh cutting of the hay had scented the air a month earlier. Only the raspberries, cherries, and late strawberries were ripe enough to pick and preserve. Harvesting the rest would come later. Plenty of time for those farming the fields around Coshocton to enjoy Pawnee Bill's parade and, if a quarter or two could be scratched up, take in the show.

Lulu and the other female performers played second fiddle to May Lillie. Like all smart producers (and husbands), Pawnee Bill knew to keep the spotlight on his protagonist and wife, May. She and Pawnee Bill led like the North Star. Although May shone as a sharpshooter and rider, her femininity was insufficient for the show's success. Additional girlishness was needed to counterbalance the hypermasculinity of the cowboys, to add the fragrance of lavender and lilac to the man sweat and musk. A good-looking woman like Lulu fit the bill.

The Native American women contributed a family atmosphere and reality as they went about their business, tending to their children and tasks in the teepee-filled Indian Village. At times, they danced, sang, and performed in the melodramatic vignettes the audiences lapped up.

Russian women added an exotic touch, riding with their menfolk in the Cossack events.

The remaining White women, including Lulu, were mostly American. Billed as "Beautiful Daring Western Girls" and "Lady Riders," they were the Cowgirls. Their primary tasks were riding horseback, performing in the vignettes, and exhibiting the skills expected of cowgirls — roping, shooting, and trick riding.

Coshocton's townsfolk first glimpsed the cowgirls in the opening Parade. They, along with the rest of the performers, wagons, and a calliope traveled from the railhead to the open-air arena. The cowgirls waved and smiled. A few rode atop the wagons. Most rode horses, curried to a fare-thee-well and gleaming like a mirror. Music squealed from a steam calliope, embellished with three-dimensional rearing stallions. A team of ten horses pulled the bandwagon. Six horses pulled a prairie schooner. All told, more than a dozen wagons and carts paraded by along with the cast members and, of course, Pawnee Bill and May.

Once at the arena, the entire cast presented itself to the audience in the Grand Entry, circling the open area in front of the canopied seating. After the Grand Entry, a program of short playlets, exhibitions, and races followed.

The cowgirls "danced" on horseback in the Mexican Contra Dance and competed in a Ladies' Race. They acted as settlers' wives and mothers in the final vignette, the Attack on the Settlers' Cabin. Individual women showed off their roping, trick riding, and sharpshooting skills. The action-packed show always ended with the entire cast in yet another procession, the Final Salute. Everyone could give a last lingering look at the performers and their mounts.

Coshocton's Pawnee Bill's show was a hit. Little girls would recall the excitement decades later as they penned their memoirs. Little boys would wreak havoc and hurt each other in the coming days as they tried to duplicate the antics of the cowboys and Native Americans.

Yet, no matter how well received the show, for the Wild West cast and crew, there was no time to tarry and no time for self-congratulation. Before the trampled grass where they'd grazed could spring back, the snorting bison were convinced to plod up the ramps and onto their railcars. Away they all went, traveling through the night, covering fifty to a hundred miles. By eight in the morning at the latest, they arrived in the next town, ready to do it all over again. Circling back east, town by town, back into Pennsylvania, they headed onward to the East Coast.

Lulu, early on, did trick riding and gunslinging. A photograph taken that year shows her posed sidesaddle on a splashy paint horse, her hair in a fluffy Victorian pouf, her dress a long dark shirtwaist emphasizing her tiny waist. A sombrero, heavily embroidered bolero jacket, and riding gloves added Mexican style.

May Lillie, in her persona as a proper Victorian woman who just happened to be a crack shot, rode sidesaddle at the time. Other cowgirls dared to ride astride in a split skirt which many of the public at the time considered unhealthy and indecent. Claims were made that the practice was sexually stimulating to females and risked their virginity (if they were virgins). Another erroneous belief was that grasping a horse overdeveloped certain thigh muscles and made birthing a baby difficult. On the other hand, riding in a long skirt could be fatal if a woman fell and became entangled and dragged by their mount.

With best wishes to Lulu from May Lillie. Postcard. Courtesy of Scott Suther.

Lulu's days that summer had a predictability missing in her prior life. She had regular meals cooked for her, a place to sleep, and was off one day a week. Unlike Frank Wheaton, Pawnee Bill paid like clockwork. Lulu also had a never-ending variety of new sights, new people, and new things to try. As she settled into her job in the summer of 1903, dramas unfurled.

Pawnee Bill's Wild West Historic Show was a mobile village. Like any village, happiness and sadness swirled through the five hundred men and women. However, the Wild West show was no cozy and sleepy small town. Working with animals, attempting ever more daring stunts to attract the public, and traveling for miles increased the risk of damage and death for the show people with their haphazard mix of experiences and backgrounds. Even May Lillie had lost two fingers on her right hand when a bullet ricocheted during a show. The danger inherent in putting on a Wild West show enticed risk-takers and those with little to lose. Chaos perpetually snarled around the corner.

A certain criminal element lingered at the outskirts of the Wild West Shows, like hyenas watching a lion kill.

Earlier in May, before Pawnee Bill came to Steubenville, the performers had tipped off the Pittsburgh police of a suspicious character. Thomas Kirby, claimed by police to be a pickpocket known as the "Chicago Kid" was jailed.

As a tumbleweed picks up dirt and drops seeds as it rolls along in the wind, the show gathered and shed employees along its route. Just as Lulu had been swept up in Steubenville, a second young person, nineteen-year-old Willie Green, attached himself in nearby New Castle, Pennsylvania.

Willie had already packed a peck of trouble into his life. Full-faced, brown-eyed, brown-haired, and short, Willie first appeared in the public eye when he became a resident, or more accurately, an inmate, at the Pennsylvania Reform School. Paroled, he ran away and joined the Sells Brother circus.

Snagged by authorities, Willie ended up back in the reform school for a two-year stint. The teenager served his time, was paroled again, and put under the care of a charitable woman. But home-cooked meals, clean clothes, and the kindly attention of his middle-aged foster mother weren't enough to quench his zest for adventure. One day in the early summer of 1903, Pawnee Bill's jingling, neighing, colorful show trotted into town, a magical answer to Willie's prayers. Like a burr on a sock, Willie attached himself to the show and was back on the road.

While no one knows exactly how Lulu Bell Parr came to be hired by Pawnee Bill a few weeks earlier, tactics like Willie's may have been part of her playbook.

The day of the Wild West show, Willie loitered about the show's animals. He made himself useful and carried pails of water to thirsty ponies and cranky mules. When the show train pulled out of New Castle, Willie was aboard — simple as that.

In contrast to Lulu, Willie's career was brief. For five short weeks, he worked every day except Sunday, slept on the show train, ate communal meals, had his hair cut, toted buckets of water, chattered, and made himself useful. By July, the show had reached New Jersey. On a Sunday, the show's day of rest and payday, Willie went swimming at Union Lake and drowned, a casualty of the Wild West show life.

Lulu, however, survived her initiation. She rode, roped, and shot her way through her first performance season. She went without special notice in the show's promotional materials. Pawnee Bill focused his publicity dollars on his wife, not the other female cast members. No hometown paper touted the story of the fortune teller's daughter who ran away to join the Wild West show.

Though Queen Victoria died in 1901, her era's standards of propriety were slow to exit the stage. Women's realm was cosseted within the home; men's realm was the world beyond the home's clapboard walls. Men made the news. Women minded the house and children. Decent women only made the papers in the social columns, the women's sections. Who and when they married, when they would be buried, and details of delightful afternoon teas covered their lives sufficiently and appropriately according to the norms of the time. Their public lives were printed right alongside remedies for cough and fish-in-gelatin recipes.

On Friday, August 31, news about Pawnee Bill's show dominated the front page of Middletown, New York's paper, the *Orange County Times*. One item was the typical enthusiastic coverage for Pawnee Bill's Wild West show's presentation the prior Tuesday.

A second article underlined the show's irresistible attraction for restless teenage boys. A thirteen-year-old Italian youth from Tuxedo Park, New York had run away from home a few days earlier. The Chief of Police came to Middletown to look for him among Pawnee Bill's crew but was unsuccessful. However, he did find a second runaway, a fourteen-year-old boy from New Jersey and arranged to have him returned home.

The third front page story recounted events which were receiving nationwide coverage under headlines such as "Dies Like a True Sioux," "Baby Indian Marches Stoically in Parade Then Expires." At least one newspaper opened with "Death still clings to the Pawnee Bill Wild West Show" and went on to remind readers of Willie Green's death and a recent severe injury to one of the show's Native Americans before describing Jose Blue Horse's fate.

Jose Blue Horse, at age three, was a "Show Indian," a "feature" of the Wild West Show. He and his parents were full-blooded Lakota Sioux from the Rosebud Agency in South Dakota. He had marched in the opening Parade the prior Monday in East Orange, New Jersey. The child had not been feeling well for a few days. When he returned to his family's teepee, he collapsed. A local physician was called, but the boy died. The county representative went to obtain his body so an official cause of death could be determined. Initially, the family refused, but once they understood the purpose, they dressed Jose's body in his fancy parade clothes. Reportedly his parents would not be allowed to leave the show to attend to his burial, so a cousin went to the morgue to take care of things.

In painstaking detail, the papers laid out what purportedly happened. The cousin, to meet traditional expectations, needed feathers. He made do with six feathers from a feather duster which he placed in the boy's hair and moccasins.

The child lay on a traditional rug and wore a miniature war outfit. His uncle wrapped an "Indian scarf" about the boy's head.

Then he asked the morgue attendant if he would be buried with any religious ceremony as the family was Roman Catholic. The attendant said the only way was if the cousin took care of it. So, his cousin, described as a tall strapping man in a red blanket, took a crucifix and rosary from his neck, placed them in the boy's hands, and asked to be left alone. The morgue attendant listened from behind the closed door as the Sioux man chanted then astoundingly broke into an intonation of Chopin's funeral march (it was surmised he may have heard the cowboy band play it), then into prayer. He gave the attendant money to put a cross on the grave. The show people had paid to have Jose Blue Horse buried in Essex County's Rosedale Cemetery.

Before leaving, the Sioux man intimidated the morgue worker with a look and the promise that he would be back to make sure everything had been done.

By the time Jose was buried three days later, the Wild West Show had passed through three more towns along their route.

After these spirit-dampening losses, the show tumbled on, rolled along, and carried Lulu Bell Parr with it. The entourage, minus the two children, zigzagged back through Ohio, to end the season with a final performance on October 31 at the small town of Pana, Illinois.

I Ain't Afraid

Lulu Bell Parr. Courtesy of Dan Katz.

That afternoon, Lulu joined a crowd at the Pana train station. Along with her were cowboys Tiger Jack and Luther Dennison along with a group of Sioux men, women, and children. All awaited the train to St. Louis. From St. Louis, they would head to their off-season destinations — Tiger Jack to Phoenix, Dennison to Denver, the Sioux to their reservations, and Lulu to Hannibal, Missouri. They had worked hard for twenty-six weeks, gathered a string of bumps and bruises, been constantly on the road, rubbed elbows with each other and crowds of strangers, and wrangled all manner of animals. Time for rest or, at least, a change of pace.

Pana coal miners, drawn by the novelty of the situation,

like a monarch to milkweed, mingled with the group. In a well-meant gesture of hospitality, they shared liquor with several of the Sioux. With that, Halloween began early and in earnest. The station agent and townspeople were treated to an impromptu war dance display by inebriated Sioux. After the performers boarded the train for the one-hundred-mile trip to St. Louis, the commotion continued.

At one in the morning on Sunday, November 1, Acting Night Chief of the St. Louis police, a Major Lally, received a telegram from Pana warning of trouble on the way. Fifty-five Sioux from the Pawnee Bill Wild West Show were headed by rail to St. Louis's Union Station. Pana townspeople had been "terrorized and the timid sought shelter" from the Sioux and they were reportedly troublesome on the train.

Major Lally responded with force and sped over to Union Station with two sergeants, two special officers, and a detail of ten patrolmen. When the train pulled in a little after four in the morning, eight policemen surrounded the coach carrying the Sioux. Lulu slipped out to board the train to Hannibal.

The sparkle had fizzled for the celebrators. Nevertheless, the police herded the entire group into the second-class waiting room where they were kept until their train left at nine in the evening.

The eldest Sioux was Chief Crow Good Voice, reported to have fought Custer. One of the young men, John Hollow Horn, was a graduate of the Carlisle Indian School in Carlisle, Pennsylvania. Hollow Horn had been a substitute player on the school's football team. Eighteen of the Sioux were women and children, including Shining Light and her two-week-old son Pony Little Star, the youngest member of the group. He was born October 13 in Ohio. Newspapers covered the interactions at the St. Louis train station and memorialized it with a group photo featuring Shining Light and her tiny son. His father Little Chief said, "Send Little Chief picture of Pony Little Star made with white man's big fire." He gave his address as the Rosebud Agency in South Dakota.

Lulu would garner a bit of publicity from the event. The interpreter for the Sioux, Ernest Runswith, also a graduate of Carlisle, carried a large photograph of Lulu according to the *St. Louis-Globe-Democrat*. She was, the paper noted, "the soubrette of the Wild West show" — a soubrette being "an actress or other female performer playing a lively, flirtatious role in a play or opera." With this unique experience, Lulu started to make a name for herself. She — along with Crow Good Voice, John Hollow Horn, and Ernest Runswith — would be back in the spring — back to the aroma of leather and horses, the cheers of crowds, and the oom-pah-pah of the cowboy band.

THE COWGIRL'S LIFE

Pennsylvania and onward
1904

I ain't afraid to shoot good and I ain't afraid to look good.
—Lulu Bell Parr, per *Springfield News Sun*, Springfield, Ohio. December 26, 2005.

In May 1904, Lulu returned for her second season with Pawnee Bill. To pique the public's interest, the show was titled "Pawnee Bill's Wild West and Far East Show."

The features were split between a Western theme and a spotlight on what Pawnee Bill defined with a very broad brush as "the Far East" or "the Orient." In his parlance, this stretched from Japan to the Philippines, down to Australia, across Asia, down the Indian subcontinent to the island then known as Ceylon, up to Russia, and across to the Middle East. Twenty-seven nations were lumped into the Orient/Far East. His program knitted them together with a loose theme showcasing horse culture and warfare.

I Ain't Afraid

Lulu Bell Parr. Courtesy of Scott Suther.

The Western vignettes included displays by a US Cavalry detachment and a reenactment of the strange 1857 Mountain Meadows Massacre. In the 1850s, friction had been increasing between the Mormons in Utah and non-Mormons. President James Buchanan's decision to respond with a show of force, sending in federal troops, backfired. Tensions, already taut as a pulled bowstring, tightened further. Rhetoric flamed. The Mormon leadership declared martial law and called up the militia. In an action characterized by the Mormons themselves as "perhaps the most tragic episode in the history of the Church," the militia engaged in a bloody siege over several days with a wagon train of non-Mormons bound for California. The militia hoped to disguise the event as a Native American attack by dressing as Native Americans and including some Paiutes in their force. They killed over one hundred members of the wagon train. Only seventeen children, all under six and believed to be too young to recognize the assailants, were spared. The decision by Pawnee Bill to include this as entertainment was a statement of the culture of the times.

On the Far East side, Indigenous Australians demonstrated boomerang skills. Taking a risk, Pawnee Bill displayed a scene from the Russo-Japanese War which was still ongoing at the time. The US backed Japan in the territorial dispute. The show crowds jeered the Russians in the vignette. At one point, the Russian performers, tired of the opprobrium, attempted to escape to New York.

Lulu found new faces among the Wild West performers in 1904. The most notorious belonged to the Apache shaman, Geronimo. The seventy-four-year-old had waged war in the Southwest on Mexicans and Americans for decades. Many had been killed and tortured by the stocky, broad-faced man. His animosity, especially to Mexicans, burned with unquenchable energy, fed by the murder of his mother, first wife, and three young children by Mexicans in an 1888 raid.

Chief Geronimo (1900 – 1910). Courtesy of Library of Congress.

Captured, he escaped the reservation three times, with his final surrender in 1886. Officially classified as a prisoner of war, he and other members of his Chiricahua tribe were sent to Florida. In an early bid for the tourist industry, businessmen decided he would be a good feature for tourists. Like a captured tiger in an iron cage, Geronimo elicited the thrill only proximity to danger creates. He began being exhibited at events. After the St. Louis World Fair, Pawnee Bill brokered Geronimo's participation in the Wild West and Far East show.

Along the way, Geronimo had learned to pad his income. He sold his photograph and buttons from his coat to the yahoos. He was kept under an Army guard which may explain the comments in the *Sun-Journal* on June 30, 1904:

> "Does he ever make any talk about his past career?" was asked of one of the circus men, Wednesday night.
>
> "Never," was the reply. "He never makes any talk with anyone — not even his own people. He is daffy and that accounts for his murderous conduct of the past. He never comes to the wagon for any purpose. Someone else draws his pay."
>
> Geronimo was seen by a Journal reporter but would not talk. His features are large, cruel and would attract attention. His limbs are strong and crooked, and his back is bent with age, but (he) walks, runs and rides with all the agility of the young braves."

The 1904 show was about the same size as that of the year before. Pawnee Bill had over 450 in his cast and again, used twenty-six rail cars. Nine tents were pitched at each stop — the arena, cook-house, two dining tents, the sideshow, blacksmith shop, dressing room, wardrobe, and menageries. All were large and they covered several acres of ground. With cast members from twenty-seven "Far East" nations, Mexico, and a variety of Native American tribes, there was no one-size-fits-all menu. The Cingalese (as those from Ceylon were called) and the Indians were vegetarians. The Arabs, Turks, and Mohammedans (as Moslems were called) ate no pork. Pawnee Bill included a Mohammedan butcher to meet the religious requirements of the Moslem members of the cast.

Pawnee Bill advertised his program as educational, clean-cut, and one that gave the true picture of the American West. His cowboys and cowgirls were regaled as people who had grown up on Western ranches and riders since childhood. The truth was often more complex.

That year, Pawnee Bill had two female headliners — his wife May Lillie and sharpshooter Princess Wenona. Princess Wenona began her career with Buffalo Bill Cody at the age of fourteen. Her co-worker and fellow sharpshooter with Buffalo Bill was the famous Annie Oakley. Princess Wenona was a braggart, or maybe just an adolescent. At least once, she was quoted as crowing "Annie Oakley is done for." Oakley perceived trouble brewing and whacked twelve years off her own age once Princess Wenona joined the Cody Wild West show. Rumor had it Annie temporarily left the Cody show and would not return until Princess Wenona was let go. Which she was.

Lillian Smith (Princess Wenona). Object ID# 70.0299, Buffalo Bill Museum and Grave, Golden, Colorado.

I Ain't Afraid

Princess Wenona's shooting skills were prodigious. The young woman could shoot glass balls with lightning speed from the back of a horse. By the time she joined up with Pawnee Bill, Princess Wenona was an old hand at Wild Westing. She already had made Geronimo's acquaintance at the Buffalo Fair where the two were photographed together. Wild Westing was a small world. Performers mixed and matched from one show to the next. At times, the shows joined together for special events and frolics.

Like other ersatz cowgirls and cowboys, Princess Wenona was not who she claimed to be. She performed as a Sioux and daughter of Chief Crazy Horse but was a California-born White woman whose parents were New England Quakers.

When discussed in the press, Pawnee Bill's band of cowgirls were lumped together in such whoppers as "western cowgirls who think nothing of a 100-mile gallop before breakfast." Lulu would not bring up her Indiana birth or Ohio residency in such an atmosphere.

Lulu earned no individual press coverage in her second year with Pawnee Bill, though she was featured namelessly in a publicity shot. A camel had been born early in the performance season and named after Lulu Temple, Knights of the Mystic Shrine of Pennsylvania. Pawnee Bill was a Mason of the 32nd degree and a member of the Lulu Temple back in Philadelphia. A photograph of the baby camel captioned "'Lulu' Temple's Baby Camel" was taken. As an insider joke snicker for those in the know, the woman holding the shoulder-high animal was also named Lulu — Lulu Bell Parr. For the occasion, Lulu outfitted herself in moccasins, leggings a fringed skirt, gauntlets, and a big ol' cowgirl hat.

Diane Helentjaris

Portrait of Lulu Bell Parr, n.d., by Frederick W. Glasier, American, 1866-1950. Black and white photography, copy from glass plate negative, 8x10 inches. Negative Number 72. Permission to reproduce from the Collection of The John and Mable Ringling Museum of Art Archives.

Lulu Bell Parr with Lulu, the baby camel. *The Frontier Guide*, Vol. IX, 21st Edition, stamped "Corsicana" "Tuesday, Oct. 15." Author's collection.

Pawnee Bill was doing quite well. As President of the Pawnee National Bank of Pawnee, Oklahoma, the papers reported him to have large packages of bank notes — ones, twos, fives, tens, twenty-fives, fifties, and one hundreds — sent to him for his signature while touring with the show. He signed them one after the other as he sat in his railcar.

A few years earlier, he had purchased as many bison as he could and developed a herd with arrangements to sell the meat in the East, including at the swanky Waldorf Astoria Hotel in Manhattan. He owned the country's second largest herd of bison, only surpassed by the US government herd at Yellowstone. A dozen of his shaggy beasts traveled with the show. Altogether, Pawnee Bill was estimated to be worth several million dollars.

As a manager, he showed the ability to have the requisite sensitivity, flexibility, and organizational skills to keep hundreds of employees — from a rarely-matched range of backgrounds —productive. He adjusted his responses and appeared to learn from past foibles.

For instance, on Sunday, June 5, 1904, an infant girl Baby Good Voice Eagle died of pneumonia. Her short life was not marked by the short shrift given to little Jose Blue Horse's death the prior year, with its dependence on plumes plucked from a feather duster and an impromptu song by his cousin. Pawnee Bill saw to it that, this time, the little child had a funeral and traditional Native American ceremony to see her off. He learned and he acted.

The complexities of life in the mobile village continued in other ways. Carlisle Indian School Graduate John Hollow Horn made the papers once again. Hollow Horn, who had been held in the Second-Class Passenger Waiting Room at St. Louis's Railroad Station the prior autumn, once more found his freedom curtailed. In August 1904, he gave a jailhouse interview to a reporter from his cell in Connecticut. Apparently with copious time on his hands, he regaled the reporter with details about his love life, his family, and his days on the reservation. The reporter from the *Hartford Courant* learned with great precision the brand Hollow Horn's father applied to his cattle. He reported snooze-worthy details right down to which side of the animal's haunch was burned with a nine in a circle and which side received the number ninety-one.

Poignantly, John shared his confidence that he would be welcome to rejoin the Pawnee Bill show once he was released from the pokey. He trusted Pawnee Bill to not only pay his wages and the fare for him to rejoin the show when he was released but also throw in extra money for food along the way. After all, the show was heading off to Carlisle, Pennsylvania — home of his alma mater, the infamous Carlisle Indian School.

When the show paraded down the streets in Carlisle a few weeks later, calliopes pumped, and camels sashayed. The reception was typical: wild enthusiasm. The schools had closed at noon so kids could see the show and avoid tempting truancy. People had begun to line up for the Wild West Far East show parade two hours before it started.

The show was sold as "absolutely clean and wholesome." The advance team often emphasized Pawnee's belief that crime is not necessary. His staff responded to lawbreakers and cooperated with the local police and sheriffs.

On May 20, 1904, "Baltimore Jack," a crook known to be a habitual pickpocket was around the show and just for being seen, earned detainment in the local jail until the show was over. Another pickpocket, "James Smith," was unfortunately caught in the act at the ticket stand on May 16. One of the show people dealt him a blow in the back of the neck which knocked him down. Cries of "Pickpocket!" "Give it to him!" and "Kill him!" were heard, and everybody who could get a whack at him gave him a kick. He attempted to crawl under the canvas but was grabbed by the legs and pulled back. He survived to be bound over for court.

Lulu survived her second year traipsing the country with the Wild West show, working six days a week, sleeping on trains, and performing outdoors in heat and humidity. While she worked, life went on in Steubenville. Her brother William still lived on Fourth Street with his wife Dora and worked as a laborer. Her grandmother Dorcas had died four years earlier. Her mother…well, her mother was around the area, somewhere, alive, doing her best to predict the future.

Lulu Bell Parr. Courtesy of Dan Katz.

LULU FINDS HER CALLING

Oklahoma
October 1905

Any girl who is able to rule a common saddle horse in emergencies can subdue a "bucker" if she has the nerve and is ordinarily strong. And, once accomplished, she'll have more real fun than any pink tea or theater party or ball-room ever yielded.

—Lulu Bell Parr quoted in *The Santa Fe New Mexican,* Friday, September 20, 1907.

Lulu Bell had an itch to scratch, a plan to hatch, a goal, and a mission. As one of Pawnee Bill's Wild West cowgirls, the adrenaline rush of galloping into small-town grassy arenas had ebbed. Day after day, night after night, performance after performance, she watched as the cowboys risked their lives, broke their bones, and sprained their wrists riding horses. Week after week, she remained one of a team of young women, relatively nameless, as reporters wrote article after article about May Lillie and Princess Wenona. Lulu would always define herself as a horsewoman and a performer.

Her thirtieth birthday loomed. It was time to take the next step.

Pawnee Bill laughed in her face when she shared her dream with him. "Told him," in her words, though he quickly made clear she could not proceed without his permission. Derisively, he said her announcement that she was going into the arena and mount "buckers" like the cowboys proved she "possessed one of the prime requisites for the undertaking — a weak mind." Women did not ride bucking broncos. Never did. Never would. Period.

Lulu turned to her tried and true persuasive techniques. Just as she had done to get her mother's court fines reduced in the Frank Wheaton fiasco, she turned on the tears. Pawnee Bill stood resolute. She nagged. She persisted. "It was many days before Major Lillie [Pawnee Bill] would give his permission, and then only after I had made his life miserable with my entreaties."

Every horse could buck, but not every horse was a "bucker." Youngsters — foals, fillies, colts — kicked up their heels and bucked in play, practicing a skill helpful in protecting themselves from predators. The occasional saddlehorse developed the nasty trait of ridding themselves of riders with a well-timed buck or two. Other horses might buck in displeasure with a particular rider or on a bad day.

Then there were the true buckers, the "outlaw horses" who honed an entire toolbox of twists, turns, and contortions to punish anyone foolish enough to mount them. They might stand docilely, looking sweet as sugar, big-eyed and innocent until – WHAM – a rider hopped on. Others made their intentions clear at the outset. Ears set back, muscles tensed, the whites of their eyes googling about left no doubt to the observant. Like criminal families, buckers often shared DNA.

Buckers were prized as challenges to horsemanship. Outlaw horses with names like "Carrie Nation," "Johnny on the Spot," and "Cyclone" held national reputations. "Dewey," the Osage nation's outlaw horse, described as the "terror of Oklahoma riders," stopped one bronco riding exhibition in 1909 by running straight into the canvas of the arena. The event was notable as the first time a rider had managed to stick to Dewey's back for any length of time.

In the run-up to major rodeos, newspaper advertisements begged ranchers to bring in their worst, meanest, bucking-est broncos to create thrilling spectacles for rodeo audiences. Shot like a cannonball from a heavy Western saddle, dragged behind a galloping bronco, squashed in a rollover by a half ton of horseflesh, or kicked by a well-aimed hoof — the potential manner of damage and death was varied. All were catnip to the audience.

Lulu Bell was unfazed by the risk. On October 15, 1905, her portrait photograph graced an Oklahoma newspaper along with those of Pawnee Bill and Sioux Chief Running Elk. She sported a checked neckerchief, a brimmed hat, and maybe… a tiny smirk. The accompanying article announced,

> *Miss Parr will be seen here for the first time in an exhibition of riding bucking horses. Miss Parr stands alone in this daring feat of equestrianism and as the cowboys roughly put it, "has them all beat a mile." She is the only woman who has successfully deprived the sterner members of the company of their honors.*

This was a bit of an off-Broadway trial run. Lulu would date her bronco riding as beginning later, the following June, with the Pawnee Bill Wild West and Great Far East Show. She described her experience,

"I made my debut as broncho "buster" at Brighton Beach, New York City, where the show spent six weeks, and kept my seat in the saddle for less than two seconds. In my mid-air flight and drop, I was pretty badly bruised, but was ready again next day. In a week I was as confident, as courageous, and as capable as most of the cowboys."

Lulu was now a celebrity. Those interested in her life learned about backstage goings on in late June when newspapers published an item about an interaction between Lulu and her fellow performers.

There was friction between the Cossacks performing in the Pawnee Bill show and the cowboys. The Cossacks had been cautioned to be more careful riding out of the arena into the dressing tent as they did so with "a careless dash."

At one performance, Lulu stood behind one of the rock-concealed entrances to the dressing tent, waiting to go on, as the Cossacks finished their act. The mounted group rode from the arena. The leading Cossack and most of his followers saw Lulu and swung their horses to avoid her. But the last two Cossacks "deliberately rode her down. The leading horse struck her full in the chest, knocking her down and the second horse trampled her, bruising her body and arms and inflicting an ugly cut on her forehead."

Cowgirls hustled over to help Lulu. The cowboys flocked in to beat the Cossacks without mercy. Lulu roused, grabbed her riding whip, and wreaked her vengeance upon the Cossack men. The melee did not cease until Pawnee Bill rode up on his horse and put a stop to it.

Touted as the only woman in the world riding bucking broncos, Lulu's performances garnered consistently flattering publicity. A year later she had become the acknowledged leader of Pawnee Bill's cowgirls. Twice daily, except for Sundays, she rode the bone-jarring steeds as they hopped and gyrated around the arena. Meanwhile, a circus fire in Geneva, Ohio led to $40,000 in damages. Lulu's future would ignite from the ashes.

A RISING AND FALLING STAR

New York City
1907

Fantasy. Lulu immersed herself in the half-truths and artifice which created the dreamscape of the American West. Rather than Fort Wayne or Steubenville, she told reporters she hailed from Wyoming or Nebraska or anywhere on the far side of the Mississippi River. Rather than a fortune-telling indigent mother and an absent father, she claimed to have been pitifully orphaned at a tender age. Like Wild West shows, novelists, playwrights, and the moving picture industry, she threw stardust over reality to create a vision of herself and the West. She understood the magic of fashion, fairytales, beads, and spangles. She was, at heart, a performer, an actress, though one with prodigious athletic ability.

In her, Pawnee Bill found a kindred spirit, another soul not tethered to a one or even two-dimensional existence. Always on the lookout for a novelty to draw crowds, in 1907, he chose Lulu Bell Parr as a lead for his latest idea, a production of *The Great Train Robbery* as part of his Wild West show. Four years earlier, Thomas Edison's film company had released a phenomenally popular twelve-minute silent movie *The Great Train Robbery* about an outlaw gang in the

American West who robbed a train and met a well-earned demise.

Almost immediately, thanks to lax copyright laws, pirated versions proliferated. The prior summer a stage version, featuring May Lillie and others from Pawnee Bill's show, had extracted coin after coin from the pockets of visitors to Luna Park amusement center on Brooklyn's Coney Island. Pawnee wanted to milk more from *The Great Train Robbery*.

By April 15, 1907, a stage — "the largest out-door theatric arena ever constructed" — was in place at Nashville, Tennessee's old Coliseum grounds. All the violence and action of the melodrama would erupt in two settings, a mining camp and a desolate robbery site. Two days before the scheduled opening, a "real" regulation locomotive engine, two passenger cars, and two freight cars loaded with scenery rolled into Nashville. They came from the New York studio of Arthur Voegtlin, the creator of Luna Park's *Great Train Robbery*. He had given exclusive traveling rights to Pawnee Bill. Voegtlin himself traveled to Nashville with plans to stay through the opening of the show two days later.

Pawnee Bill had singled out Lulu to replace his wife as the lead outlaw's sweetheart in *The Great Train Robbery*. To prepare for the stage, Lulu had spent the prior month in New York with Voegtlin and rehearsed her role.

Voegtlin, a bland-faced forty-eight-year-old, grew up in the American theater industry. Like his Swiss-born father William and younger brother Emil, he painted scenery and designed sets for theatrical productions. The Voegtlin men's personal lives were as troubled as that of a Shakespearean protagonist.

Emil and Arthur were the only children of the nine born to their mother Bertha, a German immigrant, to survive to adulthood. After twenty-six years of marriage, she left their father, William. They both moved to California where William remarried, mistakenly believing his divorce had gone through. It hadn't. Charged with bigamy, he was acquitted with the annulment of his second marriage. A few weeks later, under the headline "Voegtlin Skips San Francisco" the paper reported he "skipped town, presumably en route to New York. His departure will be mourned by many creditors."

Brother Emil was, in addition to being an artist, an inveterate thief. With the inevitability of an addict, a kleptomaniac, he repeatedly committed larceny in hotels and boarding houses. Emil was listed in NYC police inspector Thomas F. Bynes's guide *Professional Criminals of America* where his "very genteel appearance" was delineated. "Brown hair, hazel eyes, dark complexion. Wears black mustache and side-whiskers…" Convicted, Emil spent four years in New York's Sing Sing prison and, unable to reform, three years in prison in Jackson, Michigan.

Unlike his father and brother, Arthur Voegtlin dodged major courtroom embarrassments — unless one counts his first wife's claims in divorce court that he had threatened to kill her many times. By the time Voegtlin coached Lulu, he was married to his second wife. His career had moved past scenery painting to encompass acting, playwrighting, and theatrical production.

Hopes were high for a successful run of *The Great Train Robbery* in this, its latest iteration.

Pawnee Bill arranged a special treat to kick off the 1907 performance season in Nashville. The opening circus parade on April 16 would be an evening event, an illuminated spectacular. Skyrockets, Roman candles, and colored lights would fill the April night. The South would never have seen the like.

Apparently, neither would have Lulu's mount, Taffy. He was her favorite pony, named for his taffy-colored pinto coat, and a veteran of her bronco-busting routine.

Lulu, described as "but 22 years old" and "the pride of the show," carried a large flag. Taffy — fractious along the parade route — whinnied, widened his nostrils, and flashed the whites of his eyes. Finally, the gelding had had enough. He bolted, became entangled in the flag, and threw Lulu. Taffy broke from the plodding line of performers and beelined for the head of the parade.

Lulu's boot heel caught in a stirrup. The panicked pony dragged her along the pavement. Her skirt flapping, Lulu's head and body bounced along in a sickening cadence with Taffy's hooves. The screams of scattering spectators spooked other riders' horses. They galloped off down Nashville's streets. In the pandemonium, Pawnee Bill spurred his horse and brought Taffy under control.

Pawnee Bill dismounted and carried "the apparently lifeless body" into a nearby store. Lulu's first words after gaining control of herself were "Major Lillie [Pawnee Bill] saved my life." Pawnee Bill called for an ambulance to take Lulu to the hospital, but the "plucky" rider refused to go. Lulu said she would ride her pony to the showgrounds.

Unable to talk her out of this, Pawnee Bill sent a rider to fetch his private carriage and a doctor. Two cavalrymen boosted her back onto Taffy. By Sixteenth Avenue, the battered rider allowed herself to be taken from her horse and carried into a nearby drug store. Revived with a stimulant, she refused to be talked into going to the hospital. Lulu once again remounted Taffy and traveled on until met by Pawnee Bill's private carriage. Begrudgingly, she relented and was hustled to the doctor awaiting her in Pawnee Bill's private car.

The doctor examined the injured woman. He shared that he was worried she might have internal injuries and that Lulu had been badly bruised, severely sprained her left wrist, and had a headache.

The local newspaper warned readers Lulu would "probably" miss her Nashville performances as a bucking bronco rider. She'd also likely miss her role in *The Great Train Robbery*, as the girl who came to the rescue when the Sheriff mortally wounded her bandit lover. The world would have to wait for Lulu's New York-rehearsed acting debut.

INTERLUDE

Evansville, Indiana
April 1907

On Monday, April 29, Pawnee Bill's outfit was frontpage news for the *Evansville Courier and Press*. The headline was "Baby Camel is Born at Circus" and began with Pawnee Bill's elation over the animal's birth on Sunday. Then, the report meandered from one tidbit to the next — the many techniques used by the multicultural performers to wash their clothes, the trolley ride enjoyed by the Native American cast, and more. With so much of import happening in the Wild West show, the article dribbled over to page two to broadcast this gossip:

> The cowboys were busy all day yesterday running down a rumor that Miss Lula B. Parr, champion broncho buster and rifle shot, is soon to be married to Harry Wolf, a cowboy from Pawnee Bill's Oklahoma ranch and who joined the show only last week. Miss Parr would neither deny nor affirm the story. It all started when the two westerners had their pictures taken together and then went off by themselves for a gallop over town.

Less than two weeks had passed since Taffy dragged Lulu over the Nashville pavement and nearly killed her. Clearly, though, Lulu had recovered enough to gallivant with twenty-year-old Harry Wolfe.

A true man of the West, born in Kansas and raised in Oklahoma Territory, Harry Cater Wolfe specialized in roping. In Excelsior Township, Kingfisher County, his father farmed a square-shaped, 160-acre parcel of land.

The locale was redolent of the Old West with the Cimarron River and the Chisholm Trail only a hoot and a holler away. But by Harry's time, barbed wire crisscrossed and blocked the Chisholm Trail. Cattle drives had ended years earlier. Yet, Harry yearned to roam like the old-time cowboys. Milking cows and plowing for his father were not for him.

He left the farm in 1906. At first, Harry sold goods at Houston Hardware, a two-story brick establishment in downtown Guthrie, Oklahoma's territorial capital. But selling nails and varnish chafed the young man. He hired on at Pawnee Bill's ranch, but even that vista was too narrow. Harry wanted to see the world.

I Ain't Afraid

Oklahoma Avenue, Guthrie, Oklahoma. Houston Hardware in forefront. Postcard. Author's collection.

On April Fool's Day, 1907, Harry went to Kingfisher, the seat of Kingfisher county, and let it be known that he expected to soon be working for the Pawnee Bill show as an expert roper. He bragged he'd be seeing much of the United States and even part of Canada over the coming months. On the 13th of April, five Mexicans, Harry, and four other local men left to join up with the Pawnee Bill Wild West show.

Devilishly handsome, the husky fellow sported chiseled features, and dark hair. He carried himself with supreme confidence. Within two weeks of joining the Wild West show, he was flirting with Lulu and riding with her on their day off. Things heated up quickly.

On May 22, 1907, a Guthrie, Oklahoma paper reported in its Society Notes section,

> *The marriage announcement of Harry Wolfe, formerly of this city to Miss Lula Parr of Wyoming is out. The ceremony takes place in St. Louis in the near future.*

The "near future" stretched out…and out…and withered away. Despite their early affinity, the relationship fizzled. No marriage was recorded by the Recorder of Deeds for the City of St. Louis. Harry went on to marry another and became a police detective. Lulu went on, too.

THE PLUCKIEST LITTLE WOMAN

Philadelphia
May 1908

Lulu's debts to Pawnee Bill for her career and her life were large but not large enough. After five years of sweating, smiling, riding, and shooting, she took the next step in every mentored relationship. She spread her wings and flew away, far away.

Lulu Bell and Taffy were off to England to perform with the Cummins-Brown Wild West and Indian Congress over the summer. Colonel Frederick T. Cummins, touted as an Indian fighter and scout, was a Buffalo Bill wannabee. Calling himself Chief Lakota, he did cut a striking figure on horseback. His Wild West shows had achieved success at the St. Louis World's Fair and on tours.

Lulu had every right to expect a good experience in England. If things went to plan, the troupe would then tour Europe for a year or so. If things went to plan...

In mid-May of 1908, the performers gathered in Philadelphia to board the SS *Haverford*. Among the excited group of cowgirls, Native Americans, and cowboys were newlyweds Hazel and Henry Standing Bear. Standing Bear, a translator for Cummins, appeared to be quite the catch. The tall and intellectual Oglala Lakota had been a star athlete at the Carlisle Indian Industrial School. His pretty blonde wife was an accomplished horsewoman and performer.

No one would blame Lulu for feeling a pang or two of sadness at witnessing the lovebirds' happiness. She might have been sad from missing Harry if their break-up was still in the future or sad from the end of her time with him and wondering if she would ever have a fulfilling, loving relationship. But any jealousy was misplaced as Hazel Standing Bear's marriage quickly imploded.

Standing Bear had a wife and three children back at Pine Ridge or maybe it was a wife, a former wife, and eight children. Gossips varied the tale. Standing Bear would tap dance later out of a prosecution for bigamy.

But, on that day in May, standing on the pier, everyone was looking forward to an adventure. The immigration official in Philadelphia, unfazed by the Wild Westers and their convoluted personal lives, recorded Lulu's occupation, and that of her fellow performers as "artists." They traveled second class.

S.S. *Haverford*. Postcard. Author's collection.

Down in the ship's hold, the incorrigible Taffy joined 110 horses purchased from Pawnee Bill as well as a collection of onery outlaw horses bought from fellow Wild West show proprietor and rancher Zack Mulhall. Taffy would spend the upcoming days tossing his head and stomping his hooves alongside the likes of Carrie Nation and Johnny on the Spot.

Despite being as good-looking as Buffalo Bill Cody, Cummins lacked Pawnee Bill's complementary business acumen and self-control. Trouble dogged the man. He was arrested twice in the aftermath of scuffles, lost most of his animals from a $40,000 fire at his winter headquarters, and was taken to court over a missing $30,000 loan.

It was a coup for Cummins to get the contracts for summer performances. To do so, he joined with the England-based American showman J. Calvert Brown and tacked

Brown's name onto the show's moniker. Brown directed the White City Amusement Park on England's west coast. The Cummins-Brown Wild West and Indian Congress would perform at the White City and at the nearby New Brighton Tower.

The White City Amusement Park was only a year old. The Royal Manchester Botanical Gardens, established in the early 1800s and set on sixteen acres — in the too-frequent way of noble causes — had come onto hard times. To balance the budget, part of the property was leased for the amusement park. An arched gateway, original to the gardens and flanked by classic Greek columns, admitted over 32,000 visitors on the amusement park's opening day. The crowd streamed in — women with their hair pouffed out like Gibson Girls, men in bowler hats, boys in knickers, and girls with long curls and ribbons. Awaiting them were eateries, a haunted house, a water chute, music, and classic midway rides. All had been slapped together in ten weeks.

Entrance to White City Amusement Park. Reproduction photograph. Author's collection.

Forty miles west, on the tip of the Wirral Peninsula, was the seaside resort area of New Brighton. Liverpool, with its docks and ship-building industry, lay across the River Mersey's mouth. In the last years of the nineteenth century, inspired by the Eiffel Tower, the steel lattice New Brighton Tower was erected on the coast. At 567 feet tall, this observation tower was the tallest building in England when it opened. As many as two thousand paying customers rode elevators to the tower top daily. From there, they gawked at the Liverpool skyline, the River Mersey estuary, and the River Dee. On a clear day, they enjoyed vistas of the Lake District, the Welsh Mountains, and the Isle of Man. The Tower was only one of the large grounds' features. A ballroom, a theater, a boating lake, a funfair, gardens, restaurants, and a sports ground promised something for nearly everyone who could afford a shilling or so admission. Claimed to be "the finest place of amusement in the Kingdom," it was considered the Coney Island of England.

New Brighton Tower. Postcard. Author's collection.

I Ain't Afraid

The Cummins-Brown Wild West and Indian Congress was set to be the showpiece of the summer season at the New Brighton Tower. In preparation, the Tower Athletic Ground, which could hold up to 100,000 viewers, had been outfitted with tents, cookhouses, fences, and new scenery. Hammers rang out. The aroma of fresh-cut wood scented the air as hand saws moved back and forth across planks. New housing had been built for Cummins' performers and staff.

On Thursday, May 14, the SS *Haverford* docked at Liverpool with its "marvelous contingent." Lulu would experience a summer free of the incessant packing and shifting of railroading across the United States. However, she was busy. Shows were twice daily, every day. The opening parade and ceremonies were set for only two days later, on Saturday the 16th. With the anticipation of large crowds, a force of mounted constables as well as 500 foot constables were arranged to keep order. The cowboys and cowgirls would escort an old stagecoach in the parade. "Last but not least" the Native Americans would parade, their faces adorned with the traditional and striking geometry of war paint.

Opening day's success and high attendance ("many thousands") was helped along by what was described as "glorious weather"—no small thing on Britain's blustery coast.

The inherent risk underlying the show's realism was quickly underscored. A week after opening day, Colonel Cummins fractured a bone in his right hand. Three days later, a bucking bronco threw a cowboy and ended the man's fun. With a compound fracture of his upper arm, the cowboy expected to spend the rest of the summer in the hospital.

The British reveled in the exoticism of their former colony, as they had dating back to Pocahontas's ill-fated (and fatal) visit in the 1600s. Wild West shows were immensely popular and had been since Buffalo Bill's Wild West Exhibition in 1887. Even Queen Victoria had been a fan. In her private journal, she wrote of the "wild bare-backed horses" and described Buffalo Bill as "handsome." Over the years, Cody would tour every town and city of consequence in England — or at least more than 170 of them, laying the foundation for other Wild West shows.

Not surprisingly, at least one star-struck Briton had become so enthralled with the mystique of the American West that he moved to the States and, for fifteen years, immersed himself in Western life. Nicknamed the "Cowboy Baronet," Genille Cave-Browne-Cave made a living in America breaking wild horses, roping calves, and herding cattle. He even won an Oklahoma steer roping championship.

In 1908, just ahead of the arrival of the Cummins-Browne Wild West and Indian Congress, the thirty-eight-year-old returned to England to claim his inherited noble title. As a baronet, Sir Genille Cave-Browne-Cave owned an old Norman castle and six thousand acres. As a cowboy, he could not resist getting together with two cowboy "chums," putting on his "cowboy togs," and riding a mustang in the arena at the Cummins Wild West and Indian Congress "just for a lark." He promised to return.

When he did, Lulu performed before the Baronet and his party of ladies. Lulu mounted Apache, but lost her balance, and was dragged around the arena by the outlaw horse. Cowboys rushed to her rescue. They threw the bronco, lifted Lulu up in their arms, and revived her. Despite a nasty cut on her forehead and the protests of management, she insisted on riding again.

I Ain't Afraid

Miss Parr swept into the arena, threw the bucker, mounted him, and made a beautiful ride, stopping directly in front of the royal box. She was sent for by the Duke (Baronet) who declared her "the pluckiest little woman Englishmen had ever seen.

The nobleman cowboy took an army service button off his lapel and handed it to Lulu with his compliments. Lulu kept it as one of her most treasured possessions.

On October 21, 1908, Lulu and Taffy boarded the SS *Merion*, sister ship for the SS *Haverford*, in Liverpool for the trip home. Taffy returned to his dim underworld stabling below deck. Lulu had a smidge more freedom. When the wintry weather permitted, she could walk the 530-by-59-foot ship and breathe fresh air.

S.S. *Merion*. Postcard. Author's collection.

The ship docked in Philadelphia on the first of November. Cowboys, cowgirls, Native Americans, and musicians gave their names, ages, and hometowns for the American authorities to pen into their records. Lulu knocked a decade off her age and claimed to be twenty-one years old. The official dutifully recorded the inaccuracy. As a performer, Lulu had consistently and successfully claimed to be younger than she was.

Taffy and Lulu had had enough of being confined to a ship, of staying in one place of following schedules. It was time to bust out.

TIME TO HIT THE ROAD

*Philadelphia
1908*

November 16, 1908, was a Monday, a good day to meet the press, and share her news. Back less than a week from England, Lulu had been working with three cowboy buddies — Pecos, Rusty, and Big McClain – out of her rented room on South Water Street. The four had mapped out her next adventure. She planned to ride Taffy back home to Ohio, alone. As she explained to the reporter for *The Philadelphia Inquirer*,

> *I've grown awfully tired of railroad trains, especially after what I went through in Europe with the show. Then too, my pet pony which I rode during my European tour has had about all the traveling on Railroad trains and steamships he can stand. Like me, he wants to go along under his own power. I know we'll have just the loveliest kind of a time, and then think of the experience. Why, I know there will be many girls who'll envy me the trip.*

Her cowboy buddies, having left their horses back in England, must have been jealous. The trip would be over six hundred miles long, ending sixty miles west of Steubenville. She would leave urban Philadelphia behind and ride through bucolic farmland, desolate woodlands, small towns, and villages. Shaggy farm dogs would rush off porches, to bark and carry on at the soft thump of Taffy's hooves. The herds of fat dairy cows, heads down in the grass, outside Philadelphia would give way to herds of elegant whitetail deer, flicking their tails in farewell as they sailed away. Families of wild turkeys, with greeny-bronze feathers as iridescent as a Tiffany lamp, would strut across fields. Much of the trek would be through the Alleghany Mountains — ancient worn down, rounded mountains, but mountains, nevertheless. Pennsylvania's rugged terrain dictated a zigzag route with few shortcuts. Cold weather, even snow, was a part of the deal.

I know I'll give my dear old mother and brother the biggest surprise of their lives when I ride up to the old farm on my pinto. They don't know I am back. I want to strike Harrisburg first, then Pittsburg, and then branch off to Steubenville. If I can't find a place to bunk along the road, I'll just do what I've always done, picket my horse and sleep out in the open.

She would wear the cowgirl clothes she'd become accustomed to — a buckskin coat and leggings, heavy buckskin gauntlets, a big Mexican sombrero, and a "neat little tunic of oilskin to keep off the rain." The petite woman who passed as a near-adolescent would have her trusty pair of .45 Colts for protection and country taverns for subsistence.

American food would fill her stomach and American voices, her ears.

Lulu Bell Parr's leather gauntlets. Courtesy of the National Cowgirl Museum and Hall of Fame, Fort Worth, Texas.

Lulu's cross-country ride spoke of the times past, when moving across the land was done on foot or with the help of a four-legged animal. Plodding oxen carted settlers, mules hauled wagons, trotting horses pulled fancy carriages on social calls, and warring soldiers marched for miles and miles. The remnants of those days were rapidly dissipating. The first Model Ts now motored along the route Lulu's great aunt Elizabeth Foulks traveled on horseback from her Wyandotte village to show off her baby in Pennsylvania. Within two years, automobiles would outnumber horses and buggies. Lulu's trip struck a nostalgic chord and was followed step-by-step by the wire services.

On November 29, her family shared they had received a letter from Lulu. Bad weather had delayed her, but she expected to arrive in about ten days. She had assured them she would not abandon her pony for a train ride home — no matter what — and had several wagers with friends riding on the issue.

On December 2, at five in the evening, the "Actress" and "Expert Equestrienne" reached the railroad town of Altoona. She'd traveled over two hundred miles to reach the town at the foot of Brush Mountain. Taffy was quartered at the White Hall Hotel's brick stables. Lulu spent the night in the heart of downtown at the four-story Hotel Walton, also brick. With a quick step out the front door, she could dodge the street cars rattling down the middle of Eleventh Street and people-peep as she wandered by shops and restaurants.

Eleventh Avenue, Altoona, Pennsylvania. The Hotel Walton is on the left. Postcard. Author's collection.

Lulu met with a local reporter and enchanted him with her conversation. As promised back in Philadelphia, she wore a brace of two large pearl-handled Colt revolvers on her belt (and claimed she knew how to use them), a broad sombrero, a close-fitting jacket, and a divided skirt. Keeping to the well-publicized yet false background narrative of her Wild West employers, she claimed her home at the time was in San Antonio, Texas. Lulu said she came up with the idea of the trip as she, after being brought up among horses, was particularly fond of horseback riding. At one point on the trail, Taffy had stopped and refused to go. Believing the horse, who routinely performed to circus and cowboy bands, enjoyed music, Lulu patiently dismounted and sang her steed a song. Satisfied with the special attention (or maybe the rest period), Taffy resumed his travel.

From Altoona, Lulu told the reporter, her route would take her west to the little town of Ebensburg, then Johnstown, then "another place by evening." She planned to be in Youngstown no later than December 4.

At noon on Saturday, December 19, Lulu Bell Parr, in full cowgirl regalia, atop the stalwart — if at times cantankerous —Taffy, crossed the bridge over the Ohio River into Steubenville. Her hometown thrilled at the picturesque sight. After a meal and a rest for her pony, Lulu saddled up, then mounted. She shifted her weight forward, gave a squeeze with her legs, and set off on the last leg of her trip.

Steubenville's houses and shops thinned out, then disappeared. City noises of rattling wagons and children playing, faded until only the steady soft plunk of Taffy's hooves remained. Lulu headed west, out of Jefferson County and into sparsely populated Harrison County. Every now and then a lone farmhouse decorated the low rolling hills. Cross Creek flowed to her left and, running right along beside it, the railroad tracks for the Pittsburgh, Cincinnati, Chicago, and St. Louis Railroad. Her cousin Alice's husband, Thomas Bilotho, was a foreman for the P.C.C. and S.L. Railroad. He also farmed. The Bilothos' farm was up ahead at a fork in the railroad tracks named Cadiz Junction.

Cadiz Junction was never, and would never be, a town — more like a hamlet or a crossroads with a few families settled nearby. It was tiny. Even the loquacious Abraham Lincoln had not felt inspired to offer an oration when he stopped there for a bite to eat on Valentine's Day 1861. He and his family were traveling by train from Springfield, Illinois to his inauguration. Instead of speechifying, Honest Abe ate and ran. He begged off to the people gathered there by noting "he was too full for utterance."

Small as it was, Lulu managed to have an enjoyable respite from the road. She was with people who were kin, who loved her. Her brother Bill worked as a railroad engineer and lived close by in Steubenville with wife Dora. The Bolithos were solid people, respected in the community. Thomas Bolitho's father, a Cornish miner, had immigrated from England, settled in Cadiz Junction, and worked on the railroad till he had enough money to buy a farm. Lulu's cousin Alice Parr Bilotho, only four years older than her, had two children. Nina was twelve and Ralph, sixteen. Ralph stepped up to take care of Taffy.

Lulu endeared herself to the young people in the area and became very popular that winter. In April, the *Cadiz Republican* shared, in a gossip snippet, her many friends' sorrow to see her go. The paper proudly proclaimed her next destination — Connecticut, to begin work with the grandaddy of all Wild Westers, the original himself, the charismatic Buffalo Bill Cody.

TWO BILLS

*On tour in the United States
1909*

With the beginning of the 1909 Wild West show performance cycle, Lulu galloped into the orbit of world-class enchanter Buffalo Bill. The mythic man had charmed thousands around the world, from the ragamuffin street boys who lined his parade route for a free peek to Her Majesty Queen Victoria who had demanded not one, but two, command performances. Nearly everyone loved Buffalo Bill. Lulu would be no exception.

At thirty-two years of age, she was approaching the pinnacle of success. She was a Buffalo Bill cowgirl. The only remaining challenge was to separate herself from the herd of performers and shine as a star. Could she? Spring that year, as always, carried — like the ethereal fragrance of apple blossoms in a breeze — the scent of new life, fresh starts, change, optimism.

Lulu's enviable new position sprang from problems in Cody's camp. After touring for over thirty years, Cody — the Indian Scout, awardee of the Medal of Honor, and entertainer —had gathered sticking points along the way, like burrs on a walk through autumn woods. Everybody has their vulnerabilities. For Achilles, it was his heel. For Buffalo Bill…the problem lay higher up — at chest level, at his core, nestled in his heart.

William F. Cody, "Buffalo Bill" in 1911. Photograph.
Courtesy Library of Congress.

I Ain't Afraid

As proof that old age does not immunize lovers from angst, Cody sued his wife, Louisa, the mother of his four children, his spouse of thirty-eight years, for divorce in 1904. Louisa Maud Federici met Cody when she was just shy of her twenty-first birthday. Convent-educated, granddaughter of a French immigrant who was a founding member of Jefferson County, Missouri's first Roman Catholic parish, she fell hard for the Union Army man. "He was about the handsomest man I had ever known. Clean shaven, graceful, lithe, smooth in his movements and in the modulations of his speech, he was quite the most wonderful man I had ever known…"

Cody was entranced with the attractive, large-eyed, round-faced Louisa. "I adored her above any other young lady I had ever seen…Her lovely face, gentle disposition and graceful manners won my admiration and love…I thought that I made a most fortunate choice for a life partner."

Life has a way of buffeting and testing lovers. By the time of the suit for divorce, the Cody's had lost three of their four children. Their only son Kit Carson Cody died at five from scarlet fever. Daughter Orra died of a fever at eleven in 1883; daughter Arta died suddenly from diagnostic surgery during the divorce proceedings in 1904. Louisa had come to realize her husband's challenges in handling money. Her remedy was to buy property in her name to keep it away from his creditors. No longer the fresh girl he'd married, she'd widened into a rotund matron. While he roamed the globe, she stayed home in North Platte and minded what was left of the family.

Louisa Maude Frederici Cody. Circa 1913. Object ID # 2019.2.17, Buffalo Bill Museum and Grave, Golden, Colorado.

Like the rest of America, Lulu could read all about this on the front page of her newspaper. The couple's dirty linen flapped in the breeze and titillated the public as the couple wrangled and snarled in the courts. Each tidbit of their testimony and that of their employees, relatives, friends, and foes added money to the newspaper owners' pockets.

Cody's beef was his wife made life miserable for him and his guests back at their North Platte, Nebraska ranch. Witnesses testified to the friction and quoted the ungallant comment by Cody that to handle his wife he had to "get drunk and stay drunk." He claimed she tried to poison him on multiple occasions and had succeeded in killing his dogs. The dogs had been staghounds gifted to Cody by the tsar of Russia. Rumors swirled of Louisa dipping into the dark side and using the herbal concoction known as dragon's blood to recapture her husband's heart.

His wife admitted to the demise of the dogs. She claimed they had inadvertently eaten strychnine-laced food put out to kill rats. As for poisoning her husband, Louisa said she had merely given him remedies for his alcoholic stupors.

Louisa trotted out her own laundry list of unhappinesses. She claimed, with believable backup, that Cody was unfaithful. In his 1879 autobiography, he'd mentioned he was "embarrassed by the throng of beautiful ladies" who surrounded him. By 1893, he no longer blushed. When his wife dropped in unannounced at the Chicago hotel where he was staying, the front desk clerk informed her that Mr. and Mrs. Cody were up in their suite. Oops.

In March 1905, the Wyoming judge refused to grant Cody a divorce. The judge decreed, "The law of the state does not make incompatibility a ground for divorce..." He found the poisoning of the staghounds an accident and the so-called spousal poisoning attempts to be Mrs. Cody's efforts to help her drunken husband. His message to the two sexagenarians was clear: divorces were not handed out at the drop of a hat or the lowering of a pair of pants. Marriages were not required to be happy in the eyes of the law.

In 1909, when Lulu joined Buffalo Bill's show, the two sourpusses — Buffalo Bill and his wife Louisa — remained estranged and grumpy. Buffalo Bill's reputation had lost a bit of shine from the peccadillo. The money side of Buffalo Bill's Wild West was ailing as well. The fledgling motion picture industry, the latest innovation in entertainment, was cutting into his market share. In a role reversal, his prior protégé Pawnee Bill slung Cody a lifeline. Pawnee Bill, the straight arrow bank manager, a man of solid personal wealth, offered to partially fund a joint effort. Cody, creditors nipping at his bootheels, grabbed the rescue rope. The Buffalo Bill Wild West and Pawnee Bill Far East show was hatched in 1908 with showtime starting in the spring of 1909. Known often as the "Two Bills Show," it combined the well-worn Wild West format with the conglomeration of exotica Pawnee Bill had been peddling as representative of the Far East.

Opportunities seemed to be shared, more or less. Pawnee's eagle-eyed sharpshooter wife May Lillie thought it a bad idea. She abandoned the playing field and retired from performing. She would support her husband from the ranch in Oklahoma and keep her marriage healthy. By joining with Cody, Pawnee Bill eradicated his top competitor. Cody had breathing room. Lulu gained the cachet of riding for Cody, free of any competition from May Lillie.

That year Lulu became a star. By August, her image as "Miss Lulu Parr, Lady Cossack Rider with Buffalo Bill," smiling atop a horse with a raised whip in her hand, was sufficient to lure Kearney Nebraskans away from their sod houses and clapboard homes and to the performance arena.

By this time about thirty women were prominent in the United States as Wild West cowgirls. Nearly all were married, usually to cowboy performers. Most worked under their married names. Cody supported women's rights philosophically and in practice. He had given Annie Oakley and Calamity Jane world-class roles in his shows and was known to treat women fairly. He said, "What we want to do is give women even more liberty than they gave. Let them do any kind of work they see fit, and if they do it as well as men, give them the same pay."

But parity only went so far. The Wild West fantasy depended on showcasing athletic women riding and shooting as well as the cowboys while meeting the era's expectations for feminine appearance.

Wild West cowgirls did rope tricks, shot guns better than most men, and acted in Cody's simplistic playlets about stagecoach hold-ups and settler massacres. To draw an audience in a time when everyone traveled by horse, they were extraordinary equestrians. Most programs included a version of a "Quadrille on Horseback." Pairs of riders gracefully rode in synchrony to music, interweaving as if on a dance floor.

A gruesome Mexican sport was adapted to American taste. In the original game, live chickens were buried up to their necks and then grabbed by players racing on horseback. In the Wild West show, handkerchiefs replaced the chickens. Women, at a full gallop atop their pintos and buckskins and bays, leaned down and pulled up the handkerchiefs. Women also galloped standing atop two or even three horses simultaneously in so-called Roman races. They draped themselves backward from a saddle, rode standing on their mount's back, or stood on a single stirrup. They rode burros, mules, steers, and bison. The risk of injury was multiplied by the amount of time they spent performing — twice a day, six days a week, from spring to autumn.

Pawnee Bill's Historic Wild West. Beautiful Daring Western Girls & Mexican Senoritas... Wild West Poster circa 1890 – 1900. Courtesy Library of Congress.

Appearance mattered and cowgirling was a dirty, smelly job. Wild West cowgirl Goldie Griffith recalled the challenges of staying presentable while traveling from show to show by rail with, if they were lucky, a weekly night at a hotel:

I Ain't Afraid

...if we get in Sunday morning or Saturday night late, we could all go to the hotels you know because we always bathed in buckets out there (on tour). But you could get a hot bath and we'd do our washing and ironing.

Portrait of Goldie Griffith. Circa 1913. Object ID #72.0040, Buffalo Bill Museum and Grave, Golden, Colorado.

Clothing mattered. Clothing could — and did — kill women. In the 1800s, hoop skirts had cost many their lives when the voluminous fabric burst into flames from hearth embers or the bell-like cages supporting them tipped and tripped the wearer. In 1909, hoop skirts were ancient history. Instead, hobble skirts, which made a full stride impossible, were fashionable. To avoid ripping the seams of the narrow skirts, some women tied their legs together at the knees. Predictably, painful outcomes followed.

Though the show employed several costumers, the cowgirls usually made their own outfits. Their performance costumes were a compromise between safety, comfort, and gender norms. The mores of the early 20th century had no room for women dressed in men's clothing. Trousers were outside the boundaries of decency for women, yet riding in long skirts was no fun at all. A variety of solutions arose. Skirts were shortened and often divided. Early on some cowgirls inserted elastic at the top of these short, divided skirts to create bloomers reminiscent of the 1830s women's rights campaigns. A few wore pants under a divided skirt.

Wild West cowgirl style evolved to reflect Mexican and United States' influences. Big floppy scarves, western-style hats, gauntlet riding gloves, fringed buckskin, and Native American beaded motifs fit into the American frontier look. Beading was likely outsourced to the Native American women traveling with the show. Spanish bullfighters, Mexican cowboys (*vaqueros*), and equestrians known as *charros* inspired the cowgirls to wear high-domed, large-brimmed, or flat-topped sombreros and elaborately embroidered short bolero jackets. For the muslin and calico-clad girls in the audience, the cowgirls' clothing was dream fodder.

Lulu, like the other cowgirls, made her own outfits but

did so with unrivaled elan. She rode bucking broncos in both American and Mexican-style clothing. Lulu earned a solid reputation as a flashy dresser. She often wore rows of deep fringe, neat and tidy boots on her dainty feet, and wide-cuffed gauntlets along with a gun. The petite woman drew attention to her athletic body with stark geometric, high-contrast design elements. These were, at times, leather insets in her jackets and skirts. Her frizzy blond hair exploded out from her hat in an unkempt corona around her face. She tied it in back with a wide bow. If her symmetrical clear features weren't enough to lure the eye, the clothes would hold them. The interplay between her physical delicacy, prowess, and strength —scented with the aroma of risk— galvanized spectators.

Miss Lulu B. Parr, 101 Ranch Real Wild West Show. Postcard. Courtesy of Scott Suther.

Diane Helentjaris

All the fringe in the world could not protect her from mishaps. In one dust-up with a bronco that year, the miscreant equine rolled over on her, kicked her in the ribs, tramped her face, and broke her nose. Lulu healed. Papers the following year reported "but you could never tell it by looking at her."

NEW PARTNERS

*On tour in the United States
1910*

Lulu's star was rising like the sun in June, rosy with promise. For confirmation, all one had to do was grab a copy of the Two Bills' Route Book for the 1910 and 1911 seasons. Touted as Colonel William F. Cody's "Farewell Tour," it was the first of several farewells. A poem patriotically lauded the old fellow:

> *Hail to the chief! With banners unfurled*
> *Salute the "Old Scout" — the prince of his clan —*
> *Bearing our flag aloft over the world;*
> *Western-born type of the pioneer man;*
> *Hail, conquering spirit — American!*

Illustrated with colorful scenes of flags, Western vistas, men on horseback, and Native Americans, the Two Bills' Route Book documented the planned appearances for the upcoming two seasons, their dates, and locations as well as the staff.

Everyone from the eleven coffee boys to the two butchers, eleven costumers, and two elephant trainers had their names listed. Chief Iron Tail, whose aquiline profile would be immortalized on the buffalo nickel, headed up the forty-two Native American men. Leading the eight cowgirls, one of two single women, was "Miss L.B. Parr." Lulu was number one.

Buffalo Bill's Wild West Kitchen Crew Cooking a Meal. Circa 1911. Object ID# 87.0081, Buffalo Bill Museum and Grave, Golden, Colorado.

A few years later, Lulu would use personal stationery which included a header claiming employment with Buffalo Bill in 1910, but newspapers of the time report her working with a different outfit, the Miller Brothers 101 Ranch Wild West show. Articles have her performing with them in April in Indianapolis, in June in York, Pennsylvania, in October in St. Louis, and in November in Atlanta. In the fluidity of Wild West work and the tangles of business relationships, Lulu may have been leased out to the 101 Ranch show.

The Miller Brothers' 101 Ranch claimed to be the largest diversified ranch in the world at the time. The family-owned property covered 110,000 acres spread over three counties in northern Oklahoma. Six thousand horses and fifteen thousand head of cattle called it home. Twenty thousand acres were cultivated.

Founded in the 1890s by former Confederate Colonel George Washington Miller, his three sons — Joseph, George Jr., and Zach — had clawed their way to great wealth, though with a seedy underside. The American West itself had little law and less order, but more than a whiff of lawlessness floated around the Miller brothers. Their patrician Kentucky roots had become soiled with criminal charges from cattle theft to passing counterfeit money to murder. Spurred by their Oklahoma neighbor Pawnee Bill's success as a Wild West show owner, the Miller Brothers began their own show in 1907. Despite competition from the moving picture industry and other challenges, their show continued to draw breath. But the Two Bills they were not. If Pawnee Bill was one's responsible older brother and Buffalo Bill was one's overly friendly uncle, the three Miller siblings were the cousins one did not want to cross. Ever.

In 1910, Lulu Bell Parr trotted into their arena. Her career thrived, though there began to be a realization of the looming anachronism of cowgirlhood. A June wire service article received heavy coverage. "The Passing of the Cow Girl Now Declared to be at Hand" and claimed cowgirls' existence to have been merely "to maintain their influence over the reckless men with whom they had chosen to share their lives" rather than any self-actualized reason. It claimed the "few that remain are travelling with shows." Lulu is mentioned with four others and the article ends with "Miss Parr has a bulldog presented to her by King George the Fifth when he was Prince of Wales."

By August, she took on the dog-bestowing royal, the King of England, in a *Chicago Tribune* article published under the byline "Lulu B. Parr." King George V had "issued a ruling, the decree that orders the side saddle to be used by Englishwomen…that no woman mounted astride will be permitted to ride in the park or Rotten Row."

Lulu disagreed.

> *False modesty instigated both the hoopskirt and the side saddle. Comfort, and grace, and freedom of movement condemn them both. Astride riding had its origin in this country on the vast reaches of the western prairies. There it is a practical necessity.*

She went on to explain the benefits for the woman and her mount of riding astride, the positives of a divided skirt, and the joy of riding bucking broncos.

> *The best fun in the world is to ride a bucking horse…Of course, it takes nerve and courage, but I'll guarantee a few trials will convert the weak muscled, indecisive female into a self-reliant and muscular person.*

She also reminisced about her first ride on a bucker:

I Ain't Afraid

...I finally made my debut as a broncho buster and kept my seat in the saddle for less than two seconds. I recall vividly that the brute leaped in the air then shook himself like a dog, struck the ground with a thud, made a dozen swift straightforward pitches, suddenly changed ends, and began zigzagging back with drunken lurches, known in cowboy parlance as "sun fishing." In the midair flight and drop I took at that period I was pretty badly bruised but was ready again next day. In a week I was as confident, as courageous, and as capable as most of the cowboys. Nowadays the height of my delight is to tussle with an equine outlaw of the worst type, and generally the victory is mine.

Yours Truly Lulu B. Parr. Postcard. Courtesy of Dan Katz.

VAUDEVILLE CALLS

New York City
1910

Winter. The offseason for clowns, elephants, and Wild West cowboys and cowgirls — a time to nestle in with friends and relatives in front of a cozy fire and heal work-related injuries or a time to find other work. By December, Lulu had opted to continue her relationship with the 101 Ranch in a run on the Vaudeville circuit.

Vaudeville had developed into a uniquely American form of entertainment. A hodgepodge of short performances was strung together to create a variety show in theaters and other venues across the country. Admission was inexpensive. Presentations were family-friendly with no tolerance for indecency. Acrobats, Shakespeare, comedy, dance, singing, and any number of things delighted audiences with something for most everyone. All rotated usually twice daily. The acts traveled in circuits covering the nation and included entertainers as disparate as Harry Houdini, Irving Berlin, Sarah Bernhardt, Bojangles, and Helen Keller.

The "pocket edition" of the 101 Ranch Wild West opened in December in Camden, New Jersey at the Broadway Theater. Front-page ads in the local paper promoted the cast of twelve performers, three donkeys, and two horses as "America's best sports" — "rope experts, crack shots, daring riders."

Leather-hard cowboy and trail-blazing rodeo clown Dan Dix managed the show for the Miller Brothers. Born in Oklahoma, Dix had been cowboying since childhood and survived buckers with well-deserved names such as Funeral Wagon. He performed with the three "comic" mules he had trained. Bobby said prayers, Virgil followed commands in Greek, and Maud evaded every rider.

"The hardest thing we have to do in this outfit is to put stage paint on our faces and believe me, it is a pretty tough job," he said in one interview. Ominously he shared, "This is only the second week, and anyone who knows the first thing about horses realizes how hard it is to get them to work on the stage. When you are used to working on a big lot and then find yourself cooped on a stage, it's mighty different."

Dix amplified the now-folk tale of Lulu's first ride on a bucker. He said she had begged and cried to be allowed to ride and once on the steed had "stuck like a leech and when she got off, she was about ready to faint, but she quickly recovered. She has been at it ever since, and it don't take long to tell whether her riding is the real thing."

I Ain't Afraid

Miss Lulu B. Parr Lady Broncho Rider 101 Ranch Real Wild West Show. Postcard. Buffalo Bill Center of the West, Cody, Wyoming, USA. (MS6.4075.69.1 Postcard Scrapbooks MS 006 William F. Cody Collections)

Lulu and cowboy sharpshooter Roxy Mack vied for star position of the pocket edition. Mack impressed the December 12 audience in Camden by shooting with a rifle in each hand. He simultaneously broke a pipe held in his assistant's mouth and another between the same trusting assistant's fingers.

In her bid for attention, Lulu mounted the bucker "Inferno" who did his best to impress.

> *Only the stoutest kind of a stage could resist the powerful jumping and bucking of this animal in its effort to unseat its rider. In his frenzy, Inferno attempted to jump over the back of another horse.*

While the house was almost rocking with applause, Miss Parr alighted and there was a scene back of the stage... as the recalcitrant bronco continued his shenanigans. Only the teamwork of four strong men could pry the saddle off "the vicious brute."

January found the 101 Ranch pocket edition at Durland's Riding Academy's weekly meet in Manhattan. Durland's Riding Academy was a three-building equestrian complex opened in 1901 to replace an earlier facility on Columbus Circle which had burned down. The new complex on West 66th Street was less than a block from Central Park's bridle paths. The central section featured a huge riding arena illuminated by a series of three-story windows. Six hundred spectators could be seated in the viewing galleries and the musicians' gallery had room for a forty-piece orchestra. The Riding Club had elegant club rooms, patronized by riders with surnames like Astor and Vanderbilt. Riders, after elegant trots through the park in which their hips rose rhythmically up and down on hornless English saddles and their mounts gleamed in the sun, removed their top hats to sit and chat over gin tonics. Lulu's pistoning ride, the mule trio, and the other 101 Ranch pocket edition performers were a change of pace for the city folk.

The 101 Ranch cast next traveled up to Boston for performances at the rococo Keith Theater. In his week of January 30 Manager's Report for Keith-Albee Theaters, local manager R.C. Larsen typed a summary. The Wild West show was in its second week. Things "went well both performances to-day, although the lariat thrower was a little off. The girl who rides the bucking broncho had a narrow escape to-night."

Keith's by Night, Boston, Mass. Keith Theater. Postcard. Author's collection.

Lulu returned in March to New York for another 101 Ranch presentation at Durland's Riding Academy. Things became raucous with a synchronized riding quadrille which "when it was all over everyone wondered how all eight of the participants came out alive." Riders included Lulu and Dan Dix. Lulu had more to do, though.

> *The next number proved, however, that to at least one of the riders the breakneck quadrille must have seem[ed] as tame as puss in the corner. When Miss Lulu Parr finally got on the back of her bucking pony, he outbucked any pony that every [ever] bucked and it was evident that he did it of his own volition, merely because he enjoyed it. The only way to make him stop was to get his head over the back of another horse and tie it there, but it looked at one time as though Miss Parr was about to bite the dust. After she had lost from her costume everything which was detachable the pony was corralled in one corner of the ring and Miss Parr returned to terra firma much the worse for wear.*

And with that, the offseason ended. Though Lulu's name would be listed in the 101 Ranch Route book for the 1911 season, she was the caboose of the cowgirls, the last name of an unalphabetized list, well behind the Parry sisters and Beatrice Brousseau. Lulu did not stick with the 101 Ranch in 1911 but moved on.

BACK WITH THE BILLS

Fort Wayne, Indiana
July 1911

Waking up in July, after a poor night's sleep tossing in damp sheets, folks in the American Midwest often roused with a dull headache and a smothering feel in their chest. Sweltering and sweaty heat, oppressive thick air under a bleached-out, white sky slowed everyone down. An hour or so before supper, the whiteness coalesced into towering heaps of dense thunderclouds, like piles of cauliflower or stiff mashed potatoes. Cattle in the field laid down in readiness. Anyone with any religion at all knew God was up there as tines of electricity began to flit and probe around, first with little forks of tentative light and then, with rumbles and crashes, blinding lightning. Terrified children looked out their windows and silently counted out "One, two, three, four, five" seconds for each mile of distance between them and the lightning strikes. Day after day, the afternoon storms made dogs howl, watered the crops, and replenished wells.

Fort Wayne, Indiana — ironed flat by glaciers millennia ago — seemed a strange host for such dramatic weather. The town never would have happened if it weren't for its strategic site. Three placid rivers — the Maumee, the St. Joseph, and the St. Marys — supported an easy canoe portage that connected the Mississippi River with the Great Lakes. The Miami Native American nation had planted its capital Kekionga at this confluence. Kekionga became Fort Wayne. Every summer strings of storms thundered over the serene landscape and broke up, for a few hours, the insufferable heat.

Few in the audience for the Two Bills show on July 8, 1911, realized they were watching a native of their town when Lulu rode into the arena. They also did not know, until tipped off by a *Fort Wayne Daily News* article two days later, why she was hotter and even more uncomfortable than they were. Under her outfit, her "entire body was encased in bandages."

At a performance in Pittsburgh the week before, her mount had thrown himself backward. Lulu became caught on the saddle and unable to jump off as she usually did. The saddle horn crushed her right side. Three ribs fractured. Lulu refused to go to the hospital. In pain, she cut her riding time down and only appeared in the opening of each show.

Buffalo Bill and his wife Louisa had reconciled the prior year through a family-sparked intervention. From then on, Louisa traveled often with Buffalo Bill. Present in Fort Wayne, she took a motherly tone with Lulu's predicament. The *Fort Wayne Daily News* reported that in response to Louisa's desires, Lulu would enter a hospital at their upcoming stop in Chicago and stay there until her ribs had healed. Meanwhile, the summer storms continued.

Pawnee Bill and Buffalo Bill's show moseyed on from Fort Wayne. By August, rather than languishing in a Chicago hospital, Lulu was dining with her cousin's wife in Waterloo, Iowa. Mrs. George H. Myers of 622 Fowler was bubbling with all sorts of newsy tidbits when the local newspaper came to call — though amusing, not all of it squared with the facts.

The paper reported that Mrs. Myers claimed to be a relative of Buffalo Bill who was also in town but was unable to make it to dinner, though she had met privately with him in his tent. Mrs. Myers shared that Lulu was also a relative of Cody's and had been touring with Buffalo Bill since she was eight years old.

> *She came of wealthy parentage but, being left an orphan in childhood, accepted to the offer of her relative for a place in his big show...She is the last of her family as her parents, grandparents and brothers and sisters are all dead. When Mr. Cody, who is now 73 years old, completes this tour, which is his last, he will retire to his ranch near North Platte, Neb. At the same time, Miss Parr will retire from public life and will engage in business for herself, her intention being to open a store near her uncle's ranch.*

Maybe this was the stuff that Lulu's dreams were made of. That year, Buffalo Bill gave Lulu a Colt single-action revolver with a pearl handle, engraved "Buffalo Bill to Lulu Parr – 1911." The gun became one of her most beloved keepsakes.

VENICE

Venice
November 1911

"Lulu Parr created a sensation in Europe last winter by her mastery of wild horses."
—*Oakland Tribune,* April 14, 1912.

Perched above a lush brown mustache, dead center in his handsome face, Joe Miller's nose often filled with the musky odor of bison, the sweet smell of horses, and the warm aroma of leather. In 1911, his other nose — his exquisitely sensitive nose for business — wrinkled and sniffed a new scent. Like a dried dandelion head afloat in the wind, a new opportunity was wafting about. Lured in, Joe, the eldest of the three Miller brothers, changed 101 Ranch's trajectory. As boss of the Wild West show, he decided to extend the performance season. Rather than ending in Reno, Oklahoma in October, work would continue for another month.

Like a cowboy-hatted Pied Piper, Joe led his ragtag workforce over the Oklahoma border. With them came livestock, all the folderol of life on the road, as well as Miss Lulu Bell Parr. She, too, had pivoted. She dropped whatever plans she had made. Lulu completed her tour with the Two

Bills, then high-stepped it over to the 101 Ranch Wild West show. They trekked westward, putting smiles on spectators' faces in Texas, then New Mexico, then Arizona. Finally, on November 8, after seven months on the road, the 101 Ranch troupe reached their destination — California, America's paradise, Eden-on-earth, the land of fresh air and balmy weather.

Wild West performers resting between acts. Circa 1911. Lulu (right) sits with a towel on her head. The woman on the left may be Bessie Herberg. Photographic print from glass negative. Author's collection.

The decision to go along with Joe Miller's new direction must have been easy for his employees. In the past, most would have wintered at the 101 Ranch near the incongruously named town of Bliss, Oklahoma. This year, they would escape the tempestuous weather and screaming winds of the frigid Great Plains. Instead of beans and canned peaches, they could slurp fresh plums, nibble crisp lettuce, and even sample abalone. Windows could remain open and heavy clothes kept in the trunk.

Off season in California had sung a siren's song to Lulu, too. Winter on the East Coast, where she had played Vaudeville the prior year, came with an icy grimness. Chilliness deepened as the weak sun set and propelled pedestrians to hurry along the sidewalks. Furtive individuals lingered at the edges of alleys and doorways, a reminder of the ever-present criminality lurking in cities. For Lulu, after pounding a wooden stage atop devilish Inferno and working up a sweat, the cold outside air may have felt pleasant for a minute or two, but not much longer. Once inside her hotel, cold fingered in through every crack in the windows and under every door. The blessing of heat fluctuated erratically from sputtering and hissing steam radiators. California was an easy choice.

In the coming year, newspapers would report she had spent the winter creating "a sensation in Europe." Like a game of telephone, reporters may have heard "Venice" and assumed Venice, Italy. Lulu did indeed spend the offseason enjoying soft breezes in Venice, amid a network of canals meandering to a nearby sea. However, this was another Venice, an American corny and carney-laden beach resort on the outskirts of Los Angeles. It was in this town of three thousand that the Miller Brothers had decided to winter their show.

Hundreds of enthusiastic Venetians turned out and lined the town's streets as the 101 Ranch Wild West performers paraded into town on Saturday, November 18. In honor of the event, the afternoon had been declared a holiday.

I Ain't Afraid

Residents wore tags printed with "Welcome 101 Ranch" that were distributed by the Merchants of Venice, a local business organization. There was good reason to greet 101 Ranch with open arms. The show had a weekly payroll of three thousand dollars. Most of it would remain in Venice, filling the tills of the Merchants of Venice's ornate brass NCR cash registers, counted out into open palms, or lost in a poker pot. Like cowboys at the end of a cattle drive, after months on the road, the 101 Ranch troupe was ready to blow off steam.

Canal and Tent Houses, Venice, California. Postcard.
Author's collection.

Many of the staff took rooms at the St. Marks Hotel, only a few feet from the mile-long ocean beach and town pier. Lulu leased an oceanfront cottage on the beach at off-season rates. Others choosing cottage living were Princess Wenona, two of the Princess's ex-husbands, the Parry sisters, and Dan Dix. Dix had managed the 101 Ranch Pocket Edition the prior off-season.

Boomerang throwers and crack shots Vernon Tantlinger and his wife, Edith rented a cottage. The Tantlingers often took leadership roles with the performers. Vernon served as head cowboy, arena director, and equestrian director for various shows. Edith, a college graduate who had been a school marm when she married Vernon back in Pipestone, Minnesota, kept hanky-panky between the cowgirls and cowboys to a minimum. According to cowgirl Goldie Griffith,

> *Mrs. Tantlinger would make the arrangements and one end of the one floor of the building was the single girls and her and Mr. Tantlinger was there, see, and you couldn't fool that ol' Tantlinger. He could hear a step no matter how it padded down the hall.*

That winter in Venice was a magical busman's holiday. The planned town had been built seven years earlier. The architecture riffed on the Italian Renaissance. Gondoliers oared gondolas over four-foot-deep canals, repurposed remnants of drainage canals that had drained the original marshland. Known as the "Coney Island of the West," Venice teemed with honky-tonk attractions. Lanterns and electric lights sparkled along the streets of shops, restaurants, and dance halls.

If Lulu missed the hours, days, and weeks spent on trains, she could jump on the Venice Miniature Railway which encircled the town. Each car was emblazoned with a lion's head, the symbol for Venice, Italy's patron saint, St. Mark. She could watch sea lions being fed at two p.m. at the aquarium, walk along the beach, listen to band music every night, treat herself to a massage — or, for a dime, she could ride a camel.

Lulu on the right, possibly Bessie Herberg on the left. Postcard. Courtesy of Scott Suther.

The 101 Ranch settled in, rubbing elbows, and endearing themselves with the locals. When Nick the bull bison at the Venice Zoo leaped his fence and went on a tour of the beach with two female bison, three of the Wild West cowboys gave chase. After a three-mile pursuit, they caught Nick and his friends and returned them to the zoo. Along the way, Nick had destroyed a buggy and done five hundred dollars in damage to a car. For more prosaic entertainment, the 101 Ranch group enjoyed turkey dinners, a masquerade ball, a Christmas ox roast on the pier where over one hundred of the Native Americans set up camp, and a jaunt to the Pasadena Floral Tournament, later known as the Rose Parade, on New Year's Day.

If they had been in Oklahoma, the performers would have used the down time to practice and develop their acts for the coming year. Joe Miller had something else up his sleeve for them this winter — possibly the main reason they were all in California and not freezing out in Oklahoma. They would dip their toes into the emerging West Coast film industry. Joe Miller struck a deal. Bison Film Company, one of the New York Motion Picture Company's subsidiaries, would use his Wild West performers, staff, livestock, and equipment during the off-season. As a result, thirty-five Native American men and their wives, seventy-five cowboys, and twenty-five cowgirls spent the off-season making films. Bison Film changed its name to Bison 101.

California appealed to the early producers. Thomas Edison took credit for inventing motion pictures in 1873 and many early silent films were made in and around his New Jersey laboratory. But cameras and lights were in their infancy, so filming was done out-of-doors, in sunlight. Even interior scenes were often shot outside, in three-sided sets open overhead to daylight. With more sunny days and better weather, California offered an extended shooting season.

But there was another, darker reason to set up shop on the Pacific Coast. Edison's movie company aggressively protected copyright claims and did so in less than civil ways. Reports of hired thugs threatening Edison's competition were common. Bison 101 filmed a few miles north of Venice in the Santa Ynez Valley. Arrangements were underway to buy and lease nearly twenty thousand acres of land to use as a setting for the dozens of Western movies that Bison 101 cranked out for a hungry public. Part of the deal with the Miller brothers was the use of 101 Ranch staff to handle security. Few would wager against a cowboy on a horse with a gun versus the oiliest East Coast goon.

Few Bison 101 movies would survive. But for now, in the heady early days, titles like *A Western Girl's Dream, Daredevil Dick Wins a Wife,* and *The Ranch Girl's Love* rolled out. They buoyed the hopes and dreams of cowgirls, especially pretty ones who could ride like the wind.

Seven women in period costume. Lulu on the right. Possibly in the Santa Ynez Valley. Postcard. Courtesy of Scott Suther.

BRING IN YOUR BAD ONES

Santa Anita, Los Angeles County, California
March 1912

"Wanted bucking horses. We desire to purchase a few good bucking horses…Bring in your bad ones."
—Advertisement, *Arizona Republic,* February 11, 1912.

Before hitting the trail for 101 Ranch's 1912 tour, Lulu, along with other cowgirls and cowboys warmed up with a rodeo. With ten thousand dollars in prize money on the line, the rodeo organizers took a dead serious approach. Their first annual rodeo, the Great Southwestern Interstate Cowboy's Contest at Lucky Baldwin's Santa Anita ranch would be no walk in the park. Competitors would earn their money. Tough scruffy horses were shipped in by rail from northern Mexico, Arizona, New Mexico, and as far away as Montana. These horses had never been ridden. Every rider would ride "straight up" — with only a halter and rope. The Rodeo bragged that three hundred horses and five hundred cowboys were at the event.

The crowd was expected to hit 25,000. On opening day, March 9, 1912, they cheered from a quarter mile of seating as cowboys rode bulls and wild horses without spurs or quirts. Any man able to ride Snakey, a famous Belgrade bull, for ten seconds or more would walk away with ten dollars a second. No one did. Spectators screamed as one rider stood atop three horses and galloped a half-mile. The amateur bucking contest was "laughable." Apparently, a greenhorn lost out ignobly to a bucker.

Women competed in the pony race, fancy roping, relay races, as well as a maverick race with a wild steer given a one-hundred-foot start. The winner of the women's bronco riding contest was promised to hold the official world's record for female bronco busters.

The crowd was a hardboiled lot of humanity. *The Los Angeles Times* headline said it all, "Two Exciting Accidents Thrill Crowd at Rodeo." The accidents were a man trampled unconscious by a longhorn steer and another unfortunate fellow who had a horn pierce his shirt. With true cowboy gumption, the unconscious man awoke as he was being carried to the hospital tent, insisted on walking the rest of the way, got bandaged, and resumed his competition.

After the rodeo, the show opened at Santa Monica, then packed two dozen performances into two short weeks and finished in Venice. The 101 Ranch in Oklahoma shipped fresh livestock and additional staff to California. The team split. One group of cowboys, cowgirls, and Native Americans stayed behind to work on Bison 101 films, but not Lulu. She continued with the show. The heavy schedule ground on with two performances daily at times. The 101 Ranch troupe traveled the western United States with two forays up into Canada.

"The Flower of the Prairie." 1909. Photograph by George B. Cornish. Believed to be Jackie McFarlin Laird, a performer with the 101 Ranch Wild West show. Postcard. Author's collection.

The Miller brothers waged an aggressive publicity campaign. Lulu was consistently lauded, billed as "a champion rough rider." She was a rider "whose mastery of wild horses has, it is said, rarely been equaled," and who carried

> *that indefinable tang of the plains, care-free and easy in manner, riding, shooting, and roping with the skill of an experienced cowpuncher and veteran plainsman…Lulu Parr, who appears at every performance, is reputed to be one of the most daring among the cowgirl riders of the country.*

Other headliner cowgirls were praised. Tillie Baldwin's domination of the bucking horse competition at the Lucky Baldwin Ranch rodeo was often reported. The Parry sisters were "real ranch girls." Bessie Herberg, who at some point became Joe Miller's lover, performed "feats of riding that are both thrilling and unusual." At least one report claimed Herberg had won the bucking horse contest at Lucky Baldwin's. Princess Wenona, the White woman masquerading as a Sioux, was lavishly praised as "the Indian girl…an expert rifle shot as well as a daredevil rider and can shoot equally as well on horseback as on the ground."

Cowgirls brought in crowds. They combined physical attractiveness with skills beyond traditional domestic duties. Every farmer in Kansas knew multiple women who could bake a cherry pie, but few women wore split skirts and rode bison. Cowgirls also risked their lives in public.

Lulu mesmerized.

> At first sight Miss Parr does not suggest the rough, often dangerous life of the range. She is physically made in a mold that suggests daintiness, Paquin gowns and society functions among the ultra-fashionables.
>
> Many times, both on the cattle range and in the 101 Ranch show, Miss Parr has flirted with death and narrowly escaped being a victim of her daring.

She wore a gold medal which was awarded to her "by the management of the cowboys as an acknowledgement of her cleverness and intrepidity." This was given to her, according to the Miller brothers, after the Philadelphia event in which she nearly died when her saddle girth broke, and she returned the next day to successfully complete the interrupted ride.

That summer, the Miller brothers dreamed up a new publicity ploy. They claimed their top women riders were rivals. They pitted trios of their top talent against each other to win a gold medal and be the "best lady rider of bucking horses." In July, in Des Moines, Lulu, Tillie Baldwin, and Ethel Parry were announced as competitors. The competition would take place in July. Pleased with the results, the Millers repeated the competition at least twice more — in August, Lulu was pitted against Tillie Baldwin and Bessie Herberg, then in September in Oklahoma, the fight was among Lulu, Bessie Herberg, and Beatrice Brosseau.

"Bea Kirnan Trick Riding." Beatrice Brosseau Kirnan. Photograph by R. R. Doubleday. Postcard. Author's collection.

"Fancy Riding by Tillie Baldwin Champion Lady Buckaroo. The Round Up. 1912." Photograph by William Bowman. Postcard. Author's collection.

On her professional stationery, Lulu gave herself the subtitle "Champion Lady Bucking Horse Rider of the World." Whether she gained the title in the summer of 1912 or at another time is not clear, but it would take a brave soul to dispute her right to use it.

VOTES FOR WOMEN

New York City
April 30, 1913

Running late and skirts aswirl, fourteen New York suffragists strode through Manhattan's Madison Square Garden. Heading up the covey of prominent society members was Miss Harriet May Mills, President of the New York State Woman Suffrage Association, and a formidable woman. With her were Miss Portia Willis, Mrs. Marie Nelson Lee, Miss Gertrude Lee, and Miss Helen Benson. Entering the mess hall that Wednesday evening in 1913, they spied their quarry in the corner, still at their table. The women beetled over.

Harriet May Mills. Courtesy of Library of Congress.

Portia Willis. Courtesy of Library of Congress.

I Ain't Afraid

The two white-haired men were hunkered down over a meal of roast beef, corned beef and cabbage, lima beans, potatoes, and rice pudding. Maybe a little heavy on the starch, but Buffalo Bill and Pawnee Bill had survived on much worse. They couldn't be too picky these days either. Buffalo Bill struggled to bid adieu to the showman's life and the Two Bills show had continued past his planned 1912 farewell. Though not ready to give up the ghost, Edison's moving pictures haunted them — breathing down their neck and cutting into their market share.

Marie Lee was experienced in the nuances of negotiation. She led with a soft pitch. She would be riding mid-May with other suffragists through upstate New York in a covered wagon, "a prairie schooner" as she preferred to call the canvas-topped wooden wagon. Their quest was publicity, a clarion call for converts to their cause of votes for women. Far more familiar with Victorian silver choices than life in the open air, she had a question or two for this pair of seasoned frontiersmen. Maybe Pawnee Bill would share tips on how to make coffee over an open fire, how to serve supper "*à la caravan*," and other such things?

Eventually, the conversation turned to other ways the men might help get women the vote. As men of the American West, Mrs. Lee expected them to be more open to her goal than East Coast fellows. After all, women in the western states had led the way on suffrage. Tough frontier conditions left little room for the constraints and conventions of the East. Western women had early on received the vote in local and state elections. They were, if not allowed to vote in national elections, at least welcome to vote in school matters.

Over the aromatic remnants of his corned beef and cabbage dinner, Buffalo Bill assured her and her colleagues,

"Why I come from Wyoming, where the women have voted for years. The finest ladies come out to vote. Their refinement and gentleness of manner over candidates, and all the rowdy-lam disappears. That's the kind of influence for women to wield. A woman's got to be always a lady if she would keep men's respect. They are smart out in my state, though. The men used to think some sweets and a few little ribbons were all that was necessary to fix the women's vote, but they found out those pioneer women were just as levelheaded and true to thrift principles as any man. My mother was one of those. That's why I've always believed in woman suffrage."

Encouraged, Mrs. Lee beelined to the true point of her visit. An enormous Votes for Women parade was planned for the coming Saturday, May 3, in Manhattan. She had hoped to ride the prairie schooner in the parade, but it wasn't ready. The men agreed to loan the women a schooner from the Wild West show. Pleased, the suffragists pressed their luck. They had hoped to address the entire Wild West cast, but only a few — including Lulu — lingered. By the end of the conversation, an agreement was made. The suffragists would return the following week to speak to the entire cast. Five or six — reports vary on the number — Wild West cowgirls had volunteered to ride in the suffrage parade on Saturday. The women were Lulu Bell Parr, Lillian Thompson Compton, Ethel Jackson, Helen Saunders, May Griffith, and Margaret Griffith.

Cowboy performers asked to join them, but the two Bills said no. Instead, they took up the offer of five Native American men to ride as guardians for the cowgirls. This was not necessarily a ceremonial role. Two months earlier, male onlookers had mobbed and spat upon women in a Washington, DC suffrage parade. Guarding the cowgirls would be Daniel Black Horn, Sitting Eagle, Red Feather, Acey Ghost Dog, and Albert Kills-in-Winter.

Trusted employees, all had done work for Buffalo Bill since the 1890s and were more than qualified to protect the "five nice cowgirls" as they rode the streets of Manhattan.

Daniel Black Horn, a Lakota, had served as chief of the show's Native American village. As leader, he oversaw performers from the Apache, Pueblo, Navajo, and other tribes as well as his fellow Lakota. His contract for the show was typical and explicit: the Wild West show paid Black Horn twenty-five dollars a month of which forty percent was withheld until he returned to the reservation. He would be fined twenty-five dollars (or dismissed and lose all his money) if he became drunk. The final month's pay was withheld until he returned to the reservation and would be paid as a lump sum in the presence of the government agent. The show provided food, lodging, transportation, and medical care. Black Horn agreed to always appear in genuine Native American clothing.

Daniel Black Horn. 1900. Photograph by J. A. Anderson. Courtesy of Library of Congress.

Sitting Eagle, an Oglala from the Pine Ridge reservation, had fought at the Little Big Horn under He-dog. He told of seeing a group of American soldiers, at the end of the battle, begin to shoot each other rather than be killed by the Native Americans. One soldier in the final hopelessness of battle committed suicide. He "jerked his gun arm up to his head, pulled the trigger, and fell dead from his horse."

I Ain't Afraid

Sitting Eagle. Circa 1905. Photograph by Edwin S. Curtis. Courtesy of Library of Congress.

Red Feather would later turn to boxing as an occupation. In 1928, he represented the Rosebud Reservation at Fort Mead in Deadwood, South Dakota and delivered a knockout in one minute and forty-seven seconds.

Acey Ghost Dog, an Oglala from Pine Ridge reservation, performed for years with Buffalo Bill. His family always traveled with him. He lost his two-year-old daughter White Star Ghost Dog in a riding accident on tour in Britain in 1892. She remained buried in Brompton, England. Buffalo Bill wrote that Ghost Dog "has been a good man while in my employ."

Ghost Dog, Mrs. Ghost Dog, and their daughter. Courtesy of Library of Congress.

Albert Kills-in-Winter left a minimal trail in the annals of history.

The five guardians of the cowgirls, on the face of it, had little to gain from "Votes for Women." Refugees in their own homeland, Native Americans did not have United States citizenship and had no claim on voting rights. Their civil rights were curtailed in a multitude of ways. Native Americans lacked the freedom to go where they wished or to do as non-indigenous people did. Government agents permitted only "Indians of good moral character" to leave the reservation for work. Cash bonds assured their return. In 1894, Cody had been required to post a forty-thousand-dollar bond to hire a contingent of one hundred South Dakota Cheyenne, Sioux, and Arapahos for his Long Island Wild West show.

That evening, the suffragettes left the two Bills with boutonnières of suffrage-yellow flowers and votes-for-women buttons. The Native Americans and cowgirls trailed out of the cavernous mess hall to work on their "Votes for Women" yells. The women planned a cowgirl yell and the men planned to translate the slogan into their language.

On Saturday, May 3, a light breeze freshened the warm spring air. Activist and labor lawyer Inez Milholland mounted a frisky chestnut colt to lead the parade. The statuesque twenty-six-year-old had led the earlier suffrage march in Washington, DC. There, decked out like a Grecian goddess in a flowing white cape and gown, she rode astride a white horse named "Gray Dawn." With a crown atop her loose brown hair, her image became an icon for women's suffrage.

Inez Milholland at women's suffrage march in New York City, May 3, 1913. Courtesy of Library of Congress.

For the Manhattan march, Milholland dressed conventionally in a riding suit and big-brimmed hat. All business as grand marshal, she directed the marchers:

> *No talking to outsiders. If your friends won't march, cut them dead.*
> *Eyes to the front.*
> *No laughing.*
> *Keep step.*
> *Head erect and shoulders back.*
> *Remember you are marching for a principle.*

I Ain't Afraid

"Suffrage parade marching north on Fifth Avenue at 26th Street" New York Public Library Digital Collections. Accessed June 7, 2024. Photographed by H.H. Russell.

Suffrage parade, May 3, 1913, in New York City with view towards the Flat Iron Building, Fifth Avenue and Broadway. Courtesy of Library of Congress.

A quarter-of-a-million spectators lined the sidewalks as she led thirty thousand women and children and two thousand men from Washington Square up Fifth Avenue to the Plaza at Fifty-Ninth Street. Forty bands played martial music, including the French anthem for freedom, "La Marseillaise." Yellow banners appealed for "Votes for Women." Others proclaimed, "Getting there after fighting forty years," "Women are people," and "Let the people rule." The marchers included,

> *Women with snow-white hair, children not yet out of rompers, girls from Sweden, Norway, and Finland in native costume, women from New Zealand, negroes from the Northern states… Indians, cowgirls, and a prairie schooner…*

Later that month, Lulu declared in a newspaper interview, "I am a suffragette in every sense of the word…I am proud to be a suffragette." If she hadn't been a suffragette before the march, she was one now.

STARDUST

New York City
May 1913

Life for Lulu after the Votes for Women parade carried on with the syncopated rhythm of celebrityhood. Recognized as the leader of Buffalo Bill's cowgirls, "the Queen of the Cowgirls," publicity homed in on her horsemanship. She was the "expert horsewoman," "the western ranch girl who rides wild horses as well as a man," and "the champion woman rider of bucking horses." She was "the only woman rider of bucking horses and the girl who was personally complimented by President (Teddy) Roosevelt at Cheyenne."

Lulu was riding high. To stay on the cresting wave of stardom, she needed an arena, a Wild West arena like Buffalo Bill's. For their part, Pawnee Bill and Buffalo Bill were scrambling to keep afloat. Counting on publicity to beef up their audience, they had several other stunts up their sleeves in the weeks after the Votes for Women march.

On Thursday, May 8th, the Lyric Theater hosted a private midnight production of the play "Arizona" for the Buffalo Bill's Wild West and Pawnee Bill's Far East cast and crew. Over six hundred cowboys, cowgirls, Native Americans, cast, and crew members enjoyed the love story set in the Arizona

Territory. Buffalo Bill and Pawnee Bill watched from box seats. Also in a box seat was Arthur Voegtlin, Lulu's "Great Train Robbery" drama coach from five years earlier. Five of the Native Americans Wild West performers joined on stage in the last act.

The two Bills crammed Saturday that same week with other overtures to the media. They jeopardized their workers' lunch by squeezing in a special 11:30 a.m. performance before the afternoon matinee. No tickets were sold for this show. It was a gift to Buffalo Bill's longtime friend French actress Sarah Bernhardt and her retinue. In this, her last tour of America, the sixty-five-year-old, suffering from an earlier severe knee injury, no longer had the stamina for a full performance. Instead, she and her staff from Paris presented samples from six plays at Vaudeville's newly opened Palace Theater. On stage twice daily, her schedule conflicted with the Two Bills show, so Buffalo Bill created the special showing for her. The newspapers eagerly reported this lagniappe.

That Saturday, the Two Bills evening show performance also included a bonus — a real wedding on horseback between cowgirl Goldie Griffith and cowboy Harry Smith. A frisky horse had threatened the nuptials days earlier by tossing Goldie into the stands and putting her in the hospital. But Goldie was a tough one. After all, she was a professional lady wrestler before joining the Wild West.

The bride-to-be left her hospital bed on Saturday, sipped a tincture of opium to dull her pain, and put on her wedding dress. The spectacular two-piece outfit was a cowgirl's dream. Created by the Sioux women in the show, it was red leather with a beaded longhorn steer head on the back of the jacket and other steer heads on the skirt. Tiers of long fringe festooned the shoulders, elbows, and skirt. A wide-brimmed hat and bandana completed the outfit. Her horse and Harry's wore large ribbon bows on their bridles.

Unaware that Harry Smith was not her beau's birth name nor that he was wanted for murder in Texas, Goldie married her man before an audience claimed to number eight thousand. Of the wedding party, only the minister was on foot. Buffalo Bill gave the round-faced nineteen-year-old away; Pawnee Bill served as best man. Cowgirl May Schaeffer was bridesmaid. After the wedding, Pawnee Bill presented the couple with a commemorative gold medal. "All the cowboys and cowgirls rode around the arena, shouting, firing their revolvers, and throwing rice and old shoes. No one was hurt."

One week later, 780 people in the Buffalo Bill Wild West and Pawnee Bill Far East show were in York, Pennsylvania. The bright lights and luminaries of Manhattan were left behind as the trains chugged off to more sparsely populated parts of the country. But the show claimed their own celebrities.

The local paper published a far-off-the-mark story of Lulu Parr. In a mix of fact and fiction, the tale was spun of a little girl born in Pennsylvania twenty-one years earlier and taken out west by her parents. Raised among horses, the staunch suffragette was said to own a ranch in Nebraska, the only automobile in the section, and serve as school commissioner for her district. The most likely truth in the article was the thirty-seven-year-old Indiana native would be riding a roan horse named "Plucky" in the parade.

THIRTEEN

*On the road in the United States
Summer 1913*

The summer of 1913 deepened as the Two Bills show pushed on into the center of the continent, first down to North Carolina, then west through Kentucky. Fruit trees bloomed. Days and miles later, green nubbins of immature apples and cherries replaced the blossoms. Though the farms and woodlands swelled with new life, the Buffalo Bill Wild West and Pawnee Bill Far East show — the Two Bills extravaganza — was dying amid a swirl of secrets, backstabbing, and betrayal.

I Ain't Afraid

William F. "Buffalo Bill" Cody (left) and Gordon W. "Pawnee Bill" Lillie (right). Object ID# 255, Buffalo Bill Museum and Grave, Golden, Colorado.

Buffalo Bill — their leader, their true heart, the old frontier scout, had lost his way. Like a hoary old bison, his stamina was ebbing. After the appearances in New York, the sixty-seven-year-old ceased riding into arenas on his hoof-stamping, white steed Isham. Instead, he rode in an open carriage. By early June, at a Tennessee performance, Buffalo Bill introduced his younger partner, Pawnee Bill, as his successor in the arena.

Pawnee Bill's wife, May Lillie, would soon be vindicated. She had given up performing rather than tour with the lanky, white-bearded Buffalo Bill. She had stuck with her decision to live on the ranch back in Oklahoma rather than do business with Buffalo Bill. His poor business skills were winging home to roost. Unbeknownst to his partner Pawnee Bill, Buffalo Bill had mortgaged the Wild West show and agreed to perform with a circus if he defaulted on the loan. In exchange, the publishers of the *Denver Post* and owners of the circus, Harry Tammen and Frederick Bonfils, loaned Buffalo Bill $20,000. Buffalo Bill failed to repay the loan.

Buffalo Bill's business troubles lurked in the show's background, like coyotes tiptoeing in the dusk behind a wagon train. Rumors buzzed in the press. Pawnee Bill was infuriated to discover his partner's doings with the Denver men. The two Bills didn't speak for weeks.

Aware or not of the issue, the staff continued with their work. Audiences still adored Lulu, "the wonderful girl rider," "the intrepid woman rider of the bucking broncos," and "the only woman who has mastered the art of riding bucking broncos."

I Ain't Afraid

Lulu Bell Parr. Courtesy of Dan Katz.

The show's agents, as always, popped up in towns ahead of the carloads of performers and cast. They pumped up the local economy from long, complex shopping lists. The Two Bills show needed to feed staff as well as horses, mules, bison, elephants, camels, giraffes, and other exotic livestock. Like the animals, the 780 employees did not have a "one size fits all" menu. The cooks and butchers had expanded their repertoire to keep the multicultural workers happy with their three meals a day:

> *The Indians, for instance, desire nothing but meat, preferring that article of diet to anything else,*

while the Arabs lean entirely to grain foods. The Russian Cossacks like stews, while the Cingalese want their dishes seasoned [so] that another man would experience a burned alimentary canal were he to eat the viands the Cingalese call delicious. The cowboys and cowgirls demand wholesome and substantial food, eschewing pies and pastries.

The show moved on through Illinois, Utah, and Nebraska. An employee warned Pawnee Bill not to go to Denver. Rumors were swirling that the show would be seized once it reached Denver, home of Cody's unsatisfied creditors Tammen and Bonfils. But Pawnee Bill stubbornly kept to the scheduled course. Once there, in the mile-high city, the first performance was uneventful.

On July 21, the cast made their grand entry as usual. Horses shone and sparkled, the result of fastidious currying, brushing, and polishing. Cowboys and cowgirls grinned, their fringe feathering and floating in the air as their horses trotted and cantered. Lakota brandished spears and rode with unfettered grace. The crowd clapped and cheered. Parents nodded at their children, proud to have the financial wherewithal to share such fun with them.

I Ain't Afraid

Lakota men on horseback racing in arena. Object ID # 87.0060, Buffalo Bill Museum and Grave, Golden, Colorado.

Pawnee Bill peeped from behind the backdrop, making sure all was well. It wasn't. A hand dropped down on his shoulder. He turned around and faced six Denver sheriffs. Their message to the entrepreneur: his show was seized and no longer his to run. The hammer had dropped, heartlessly. Not only was the six thousand dollars from that day's ticket sales confiscated but also all the rest of the show's money and equipment. Even the employees' costumes, street clothes, and personal possessions were taken, leaving them with only the clothes they were wearing and the money in their pockets. Newspaper reports estimated three to five hundred Two Bills show employees were stranded in Denver without any means of support.

Buffalo Bill had a practice of paying, while on the road, only the husbands of the married couples employed by the Wild West show. Wives' wages were held aside and paid at the end of the season. For newlywed Goldie Griffith, this meant:

> *...well, you see you got paid every week but uh the women, this was the idea, us married couples we would leave our money in the wagon and let the husbands draw their money out and we would use that for the whole season and then we would have stake when the season was over. Well, that's what happened down here in Denver when they cashed the wagon...they tied up everything. They tied up what we called our street trunks what's got our street clothes in you know and they tied up our wardrobe...they confiscated everything.*

Goldie talked herself into a job as a mule skinner — driving a six-mule team pulling a water wagon. She drove the team nine trips a day, filling the water tank at the Overland Hotel and talking the mules into pulling it two blocks to get water to the show's livestock. Her pay was a dollar a day, five days a week and paid by the court-appointed managers of the show. Her new groom earned the same amount helping with the livestock.

Even Pawnee Bill was not immune. He had to sue in federal court to regain what was due him: his saddle and traveling trunk, the only items returned to his home in Oklahoma.

In the immediate aftermath of the show's seizure, the livestock was moved to the stable in Denver's Overland Park.

I Ain't Afraid

A few days later, the performers joined them and slept in the stalls on beds of hay. With only the clothes they were wearing when the sheriffs confiscated everything, they'd rinse out what they could at night and hope it dried by morning. Food was sketchy, though Buffalo Bill raised five hundred dollars which all went to feed them. Folks pooled the scant money they had and decided the priority was to get the Native Americans and children home. Some of the Native Americans sold their costumes to get enough funding to make it to their reservations.

A troupe of boys who had performed as Boy Scouts walked home to Chicago from Denver. They began walking in late August and soon ran out of funds, but by giving exhibition drills as barter for food and a place to sleep, they made it home on October 14.

Pawnee Bill, said to have the personal wealth to satisfy the show's debts, chose instead to join his wife on their ranch. He would sum up his feelings later, after Buffalo Bill's passing, as "Time smooths everything. Buffalo Bill died my friend. He was just an irresponsible boy."

On August 21, the Buffalo Bill Wild West and Pawnee Bill Far East show's property was sold at public auction. Buffalo Bill refused to attend as he did not want to witness the auctioning of Isham, the white horse he had ridden for over twenty years. His valet, Carlo Miles, and Colonel C. J. Bills, one of Buffalo Bill's many friends, bid the horse up to one hundred and fifty dollars. Miles, in tears as he reached the limit of his budget, whispered to a friend, "If the man who buys that horse don't give him back to Colonel Cody, I'll steal the horse tonight and take it to him." Unaware of Miles's plan, Colonel Bills gave Isham back to Buffalo Bill.

Lulu Bell made her way to Cheyenne, Wyoming. At the

end of August, she exhibited on behalf of the Buffalo Bill show in Cheyenne's Frontier Days, her appearance as the show's representative arranged before the debacle in Denver. What began in the late 1800s as a one-day round-up had grown to a multi-day outdoor rodeo and western celebration. The local paper reported "The stars of the ladies' rough riding exhibition were Minnie Thompson and Miss Lulu Parr late of the Buffalo Bill Show. Miss Parr made a fine ride on Kangaroo, but no better than the Thompson girl who rode Madame X." Lulu, "the Buffalo Bill champion," also rode the bucker Red Sandy in the ladies' bucking bronco exhibition.

Things were looking up.

"Lulu B. Parr riding a broncho, Aug. 20 – 23, Cheyenne, Wyo." 1913. Lulu on Kangaroo at the 1913 Frontier Days in Cheyenne.

LULU AND THE MULHALLS

Salt Lake City, Utah
September 1, 1913

Five hundred souls slept soundly to the rhythm of the rails as the two long trains rolled through the great valley. The cars were double-length, circus cars, made to carry the most exotic of cargos to the most ordinary of towns and hamlets on the continent. Ahead the ridge of the Wasatch Mountains loomed in a black huddle against the night sky, like a covey of gossiping crows. The Native American families slumbered on flat cars blanketed by drifts of glittering stars. In the sleeper cars, the other performers of Zack Mulhall's Oklahoma Ranch Wild West show dreamed of sweethearts, horses, guns, and lariats amid the familiar scent of their colleagues. Movement stopped after the trains clattered into Salt Lake City in the middle of the night. For a few hours, livestock and humans slept in the still air until roused by the dawn and the shouts of the workmen pitching their billowing tents.

Riding her pony in the parade that first day in September was one of "the most famous" performers, "the champion girl broncho buster," Miss Lulu Parr. Sharply dressed as always, her big hat was angled to capture the eyes of the crowds along the parade route. She handled the reins with economy and sat as one with the horse.

After showing off her equestrian prowess at Cheyenne's annual rodeo, Lulu had hitched her star to Mulhall's Wild West for the end of the season. She was lucky. Others left high and dry by the abrupt death of the Two Bills show were still struggling to recover. Sixteen boys from the group that had performed as scouts were approaching Nebraska on their trek by foot from Denver to Chicago and wouldn't make it home until six weeks in the future. They had managed to scrape up enough money to send a few of the younger ones ahead by train. Goldie Griffith was still in Denver, skinning mules and caring for the Two Bills' animals. Though the Oklahoma Ranch Wild West was not as big as the Two Bills or 101 Ranch shows, it was a job.

With her decision to work for Zack Mulhall, Lulu stepped into the realm of a clan with powerful connections and a unique vision of family. Zack Mulhall rose to prominence after a precarious, teetering start in life. Born Zachariah Vandeveer in Missouri to a well-off farmer, his family moved to Texas to seek their fortune in the cattle business. Zack's mother died soon after the move. Zack was seven. Three years later, his father drove a herd of cattle to New Orleans to sell them. He and several others on the cattle drive came down with yellow fever in New Orleans and died there. Orphaned, ten-year-old Zack was taken in by his mother's sister Susan Mulhall and raised in St. Louis.

The prosperous Mulhalls owned a meat packing plant. They welcomed Zack into their already large family with an open heart, though they did not formally adopt him. They also took in their niece Mary Agnes Locke to raise. The children received a Roman Catholic education. Zack eventually enrolled in the college later known as Notre Dame.

I Ain't Afraid

Mary Agnes flourished at St Mary's of the Woods Academy, excelling in arts and science, and becoming a talented pianist. She grew up to be described as a beautiful, elegant woman. Zack dropped out twice, never graduated, and went to work for the ATF, the Atchison, Topeka, and Santa Fe railway.

At twenty-one, he married Mary Agnes Locke, the woman he'd been raised with, and they created a home in St. Louis. They would have eight children together but only two would reach adulthood.

At first, Zack ferried cattle across the Mississippi. Eventually, he became responsible for the transportation of all cattle carried in the area west of the Mississippi by the Atchison, Topeka, and Santa Fe. He roamed cattle country, throughout Kansas, Oklahoma, and Texas — learning the ins and outs of the business, becoming familiar with the cattlemen, and building up his own cattle business on the side.

When Oklahoma opened to settlement, Zack competed in the land race of 1889. He gained his chosen spot adjacent to an ATSF railhead. This became the town of Mulhall.

Referred to in contemporary newspapers as the "Father of Oklahoma," Zack had strong ties with that cowboy wannabe and U.S. President, Theodore Roosevelt. Zack's daughters, Lucille and Bossie, charmed the politician with their roping and riding. Roosevelt accompanied Zack on hunting forays, stayed at Zack's ranch, and reciprocated by hosting the Mulhalls at the White House and having Bossie ride in his inaugural parade. Rumors that Roosevelt would appoint Zack Oklahoma Territorial Governor floated about but did not come to fruition.

Inspired by the success of the nearby Miller Brothers' 101 Ranch Wild West show, Zack entered the business in 1900. Never as successful as Buffalo Bill or the Miller Brothers, he nevertheless managed to groom tomboy Lucille into national prominence as the epitome of cowgirlhood. Often erroneously claimed to be the first woman called a cowgirl, Lucille became an expert horse trainer, trick rider, and roper. Blonde and girlish, she competed successfully against men in steer roping, hunted coyotes, and taught her horse Governor Ferguson to do everything except write in cursive.

> *Every day for two hours, Lucille worked with her horse Governor…She didn't allow anyone else to handle him…at a command, he learned to pick up a wooden handle dinner bell with his mouth and swing his head while the bell rings; given another command, he would sink down on his back legs and sit upright like a dog. He learned to play lame and hobble around, favoring one leg at a time. He could bow to an audience, dance to music, rear on his hind legs, and walk on his knees.*

When Lulu joined the show, Zack was sixty-five with no evidence of slowing down. Strong-willed, even domineering, he narrowly escaped a three-year prison sentence on the charge of assault to kill. In 1904, at the St. Louis World's Fair, Zack shot a man during an altercation. The man followed an unspoken code of the West and did not press charges. Shooting in a crowded street scene is always risky and another of Zack's bullets seriously injured a young bystander who was not a forgiver. He pursued his case and initially won. Zack was never imprisoned, and the case was dropped on a technicality two years after his conviction.

On her part, Lulu had rubbed shoulders with roughneck cowboys, cowmen, and managers for years. She did her job riding outlaw horses for Zack Mulhall, her portrait graced newspaper ads for the show. She made plans for the coming offseason which held personal as well as professional promise.

In October, 101 Ranch part-owner and manager, Edward Arlington bragged to the press of his success in engaging Lulu and other high-level performers for a South American junket during the offseason. Most of the talent was from the 101 Ranch or Buffalo Bill shows. He and a theatrical agent Roy Chandler, who was based in South America and had lived in Buenos Aires for twenty years, created the small Arlington and Chandler Wild West show for the tour.

At the time, Chandler was busy arranging for several American programs to travel to the Southern Hemisphere. The Wild West show held particular opportunities for success. South America had its own vibrant cowboy and horse cultures. Movies about the American West had received enthusiastic reception. Additionally, former rancher and Rough Rider, Teddy Roosevelt would be visiting during the same period, potentially piquing further interest in the United States.

Roosevelt planned to give speeches in Argentina and Brazil and then lead a scientific expedition into the continent's humid and incompletely mapped interior. Chandler and Arlington were coordinating their efforts with the former president's tour. Chandler, his Wild West advance team, Roosevelt, and the Roosevelt cadre would travel together down south in October. The remainder of the Arlington and Chandler Wild West troupe would follow a few weeks later.

On the personal side, Lulu Bell had other things to consider, or at least other men – namely Zack's son Charles Joseph Mulhall. Twenty-five-year-old Charley rode broncos in his father's Wild West show. He glowed with healthy good looks. Fair-haired and square-jawed, he had the erect posture and grace of a natural athlete. The fellow perched his hat atop his curly head with panache.

Promotional posters showed handsome Charley alongside the rest of his purported family – his father Zack and his sisters Lucille, Georgie, and Mildred. However, the facts behind the poster were much more convoluted than the public would reasonably expect.

The Mulhall Family. Top (from left to right): Lucille Mulhall, Zack Mulhall, Mildred Mulhall. Bottom left: "Georgie," i.e. Mary Smith, Charley Mulhall's mother. Bottom right: Charley Mulhall. Clipping from unidentified newspaper. Public domain.

True, Zack was his father. From there, the family story took on a gothic silhouette. The attractive brunette labeled

I Ain't Afraid

"Georgie" in the poster was not Zack's daughter, but his longtime lover Mary Smith. About ten years into his marriage with Mary Agnes, as he roved cattle country in his work for the railroad, a waitress in Kansas caught his attention and then, his heart. Zack became enthralled with the dark-haired, buxom teenager Mary Smith. Charley was their first child.

After gaining his land in the Oklahoma land rush and moving his wife Mary Agnes and his legitimate children out to the ranch, Zack installed Mary Smith and Charley in his home in St. Louis. The neighbors believed Zack and Mary Smith were married.

Mary Smith became pregnant a second time. After she gave birth to their daughter, Zack brought her and her unnamed baby to his ranch in Oklahoma. He explained to his wife that Mary Smith was an unwed mother in need of help. He had Mary Smith give up her baby girl to Mary Agnes. He gave his wife the privilege of naming the baby. She named her Mildred Madeline after her twins Mildred and Madeline who had died at birth. She raised the baby as her own. Mary Smith returned to St. Louis. She would later tell Charley and Mildred that giving up her daughter was the hardest thing she ever did.

Several years later, after the death of his last legitimate son, Zack brought Mary Smith and ten-year-old Charley to live on the ranch in Mulhall, Oklahoma. He planned to develop Charley into a Wild West star alongside his half-sisters, Bossie and Lucille. Mary Smith joined the Wild West show crew as "Georgia Mulhall" and masqueraded before the public as a sibling to her children Mildred and Charley and to Zack's legitimate daughter, Lucille.

Mary Agnes figured out quickly that Zack and "Georgia" had a sexual relationship. After this discovery, Mary Smith/

Georgia spent a great deal of her time on the road, promoting the Wild West show and keeping out of Mary Agnes's line of vision. Charley, of course, at ten, knew exactly who Zack, Georgia, and Mildred were. As a teen, he spilled the beans to his sister as to Georgia's true identity.

Charley Mulhall had been charming females for years. A fourteen-year-old girl he met at a 1908 Fourth of July celebration was "captivated by the manly bearing and excellent horsemanship of the youth." Within a few months, twenty-year-old Charley snatched two of his father's best horses as well as the smitten adolescent girl. The two rode off into the night. Newspapers reported with a chuckle, "It is said that Col. Mulhall is saying little but thinking much, while the mother of the girl is both saying and thinking a whole lot of things." The mother, a schoolteacher, correctly guessed where the two were headed and hopped a train to Ponca City, Oklahoma. She arrived in time to thwart their planned marriage.

In 1909, Goldie Griffith — the same Goldie who would later work with Lulu —was performing as a lady wrestler at the Appalachian Exposition in Memphis. Charley was riding broncos with his father's Wild West show at the Exposition. Goldie met the charmer, and he took her breath away — an infatuation from which she would never recover.

> *That's when I decided that I was going to be a cowgirl...I always liked horses and I'd ride one every time I'd seen it...and then Charley Mulhall kind of talked me into why didn't I become a cowgirl...I was stuck on a cowboy [Charley Mulhall], so I thought I'd better learn to ride... I'm glad I didn't marry him though.*

I Ain't Afraid

Lulu did marry Charley. Within two months of her Salt Lake City appearance and less than a month before her thirty-sixth birthday, she and Charley were united as husband and wife. The nuptials were Saturday, October 25, at St. Paul's Presbyterian Church in St. Louis, Missouri.

ASEA

Brooklyn
November 1, 1913

The SS *Vasari* slipped out from Brooklyn's Pier 9 and swung into the East River. Passengers hung over the rails to wave a last goodbye to their kin and friends on shore. Overhead loomed the Brooklyn Bridge. Its powerful spiderwebs of steel hung from slotted stone towers supporting the bridge's deck. Pedestrians, horse-drawn carriages, and trains bustled back and forth attending to their Saturday needs. With the island of Manhattan to starboard and Brooklyn on its port side, the ocean liner nosed past the Statue of Liberty. New York grew smaller and smaller as the ship steamed off to Buenos Aires, Argentina.

I Ain't Afraid

S.S. *Vasari*. Postcard. Author's collection.

The waves became choppy. Cold November winds buffeted the passengers still at the rails. As the view grew less interesting, they drifted off to their berths or the overstuffed chairs in the smoking room. An impressive ship, the *Vasari* had been built in 1908 to replace the SS *Velasquez* which had been lost off the coast of Brazil to a hellacious combination of high seas, thick fog, and rocks. Until 1913, the *Vasari* was British shipping company Lamport & Holt's largest and most luxurious ship on the New York-to-Argentina route. However, its footprint of 485 by 59 feet made it only forty yards longer than an American football field and one-third as wide. This would be the entire world for the passengers as they traveled for twenty-five days to the Southern Hemisphere.

Lamport & Holt playing card. Author's collection.

As planned, manager Roy Chandler had sailed ahead on another of Lamport & Holt's v-class ships, the *Vandyck*. He accompanied Teddy Roosevelt and the Roosevelt retinue comprised of his wife, his son Kermit Roosevelt, and his expedition team.

Ed Arlington and the show's advance men were also on board, ready to plaster posters, place ads, and drum up excitement. Arlington had brought his daughter and wife, both actresses, along for the tour.

A total of seventy-four people connected with the Arlington and Chandler Wild West traveled on the *Vasari*. Lulu had worked with most, if not all of them, in the decade since she stepped into the Wild West show universe. They included Beatrice Brosseau, Edith Tantlinger, her husband Verne, and headliner Bill Pickett. Pregnant, just months after her Madison Square Garden marriage on horseback, Goldie Griffith stayed Stateside with her mother. But her wanted-for-murder husband was on the tour, working as one of cowboys under his assumed name of Harry Smith. Ten Native Americans with four of their children were in the troupe.

One person, however, was missing: Charley Mulhall, Lulu's husband. Married a week earlier, the newlyweds' marriage notice had been published in the *St. Louis Post-Dispatch* on Monday — which was the last day the couple spent together. Once again, the dream of marital happiness had slipped away from Lulu. According to Lulu, Charley hightailed it out of her life after three days of marriage, never to return, and never to provide financial support for her.

Marriages implode for any number of reasons. Charley was a man of action — impetuous and charming. For those willing to make a guess, one likely explanation is that Charley once again did something on his own, not in his domineering father Zack's game plan, and his father quickly jerked him back into his realm of control. Remember: Zack had the personal power, nerve, and poor judgment to talk his mistress into surrendering her infant to his wife and to talk his wife into raising the child.

Zack had other plans for Charley, his only surviving son, than a life with Lulu Bell Parr.

Instead of canoodling with his bride on a cruise into the Southern Hemisphere's summer, the groom and his little sister Mildred were appearing in half-sis Lucille's traveling vaudeville show.

On the 18th of November, their performance in Chicago

would be punctuated by extra excitement when Lucille's longhorn steer Petty went rogue, stumbled off the stage, and fell into the first two rows of seats. No one was hurt. Life went on for winsome Charley. He had promised to get Lulu a position with Lucille's show. That promise proved as empty as his marriage vows. Lulu would have over three weeks aboard the SS *Vasari* to marinate in her misery if she so chose.

No one would have blamed any of the passengers if they felt a *frisson* of anxiety as the *Vasari* steamed south. No number of chintz chairs in the smoking parlor and overwrought meals could erase from their minds the sinking of the *Titanic* the prior year with the loss of well over one thousand souls. Holt & Lamport, as venerable as the company was, had lost one of its luxury liner ships earlier in the year. It succumbed off the coast of Portugal to the triple whammy of rocks, thick fog, and heavy seas. Though over two hundred people were rescued in efforts lasting four days, between twenty-seven and thirty-eight perished. It didn't help that Lulu's ship, the *Vasari,* was leaving port on November 1 – All Saints Day, *El Día de los Muertos* – a day associated with the dead across many cultures. Maybe the nervous travelers consoled themselves with the knowledge that they were not traveling in iceberg country.

Chief of the Cowboys Milt Hinkle summed up the trip in this way:

> *It proved to be a bad voyage, as the ocean was very rough. The trip was made in twenty-five days. Harry Smith, the cowboy who had been shot in the hip in Houston,* [by police seeking to arrest him for the murder charge] *was with us. After Goldie had dug the .38 slugs out of his leg with a*

penknife, she brought him by train to New York and stayed to see him off. I was glad to see Harry again…About five days out from New York, one of the Indians broke out with a bad case of smallpox. All of the top performers sailed first class; some of the single cowboys, second class; but the Indians rode steerage, far down in the hold. Most of the Indians took down with the "pox."

The ocean got very rough, and we had lots of seasickness. Hank Durnell, one of America's greatest trick riders and ropers took smallpox and begged to be thrown overboard, he was so sick. Four of the Indians died. The crew sewed them up in canvas and slid them overboard, far away from their hunting grounds.

SOUTH AMERICA

Buenos Aires, Argentina
November 29, 1913

After a few stops on the coast of South America, the ship pulled into Buenos Aires, Argentina. Arlington managed to duck any quarantine or isolation requirements by the health inspectors. Some say he bribed the officials. Hinkle recalled the Native Americans covering their heads and faces with their blankets to avoid detection of the well-known lesions of active smallpox. Both might be true.

The livestock did not fare as well. A yellow trick-riding horse belonging to cowboy Otto Kline was, according to the Argentinean inspectors, sick with glanders. To avoid spreading the bacterial disease — a disease mostly of horses, donkeys, and mules, though it can sicken humans — all forty-eight of the trained show horses needed to be killed, then their bodies burned.

Arlington attempted to negotiate.

> *In spite of everything I could do, the horses were ordered to be shot...I went to the charge d'affaires of the United States, but he was powerless to assist me. The horses first were held for eight*

> days, then thirty days more. That took all our time in Argentina, and we were obliged to cancel our dates. I agreed to rent a pasture in an isolated part of the country and keep the animals there, but the authorities turned a deaf ear.
>
> I was obliged to buy Argentina horses and break them in. They have a fine quality of horses there, a sort of polo pony type, and they were easy to train. We bought fifty of them and they proved satisfactory.

While the show was getting set up to open in Buenos Aires's Park of the Japanese, Hinkle, Harry Smith, and another cowboy had traveled out to cattle and horse country and bought the replacement stock, including a small mule for the show's clown to train. Hinkle claimed to have reconnected with Butch Cassidy's sidekick Kid Curry while out on the Argentinean grasslands, the *pampas*.

The show opened on a Sunday, giving three performances to packed houses characterized as "enormous business" and "a huge success." According to Hinkle, "The newspaper gave us lots of good publicity in the next morning's edition, so the show was making money…Lulu Bell Parr, one of the cowgirls with the Buffalo Bill Show, made a big hit riding a bucking horse." Jane Fuller and Beatrice Brosseau shared later that the head of Argentina, President Alcorta, called them to his box at the end of the first performance and gave each a decorated and jeweled gold coin hung as a pendant on a gold bead necklace.

Verne Tantlinger reported back to American newspapers that the Argentinean government had "squared things" by taking 20,000 school children to the Wild West show "to illustrate how the North Americans do things." Rancher Pedro Casey invited Hinkle and others out to his ranch for a get-together and gifted him with fourteen horses. Hinkle gave one of them to Beatrice Brosseau. He gave another, "a little roan and the best show horse I ever saw," to Lulu. She shipped it back to the States and rode it in performances for years.

A staff worker sent a postcard home in January saying the troupe was putting on three to five shows daily in Buenos Aires.

The adventures continued as the Arlington and Chandler Wild West made its way through South America. While performing in Rio de Janeiro, Brazil, the country's president declared martial law. Brazilians had protested his marriage to a much younger woman. Several people were shot in the uproar. Concerned that Brazilians might get weapons at the Wild West show, the military searched the spectators as they left the performances.

HEADING BACK

Rio de Janeiro, Brazil
March 11, 1914

By March, the show had finished its run in South America. On March 11, Lulu boarded the SS *Vasari* in Rio de Janeiro. She was one of seven "Saloon" passengers — later termed "first class" passengers — traveling from Rio to the Caribbean island of Trinidad. They included Ed Arlington's wife and daughter, the Tantlingers, and Roy Chandler. Rather than return directly to the States, Lulu and some of the performers made a stopover to perform in Trinidad. Ed Arlington was also on the ship, but he would sail on to New York without lingering in Trinidad.

Each Saloon passenger received a sixteen-page pamphlet, *Lamport & Holt Line: List of Passengers.* Handsomely printed on heavy cream stock with a gold tasseled cord, it included such information as the cost for a shampoo by the ship's barber, the times of day the bell or bugle announced meals, and who to contact to arrange for a change in seating at the table.

Passenger List for S.S. *Vasari* sailing Thursday, March 5, 1914, from Buenos Aires. Lulu is listed (along with the Tantlingers, R. Chandler, and Ed Arlington's wife and daughter) as a Saloon passenger, schedule to sail from Rio de Janeiro and debark in Trinidad. Ed Arlington is listed as sailing on to New York. Photograph by author. Author's collection.

Meals were elaborate. The *Vasari* dinner menu for the night it left Buenos Aires for Rio, for example, was a masterpiece of British snobbery. *Sole frite à l'Anglaise, côtelette de mouton, jardinière,* roast gosling, *tête de veau à la Cavours,* forced green peppers, Horton's ice cream, *café noir,* and thirteen other dishes tempted the travelers.

I Ain't Afraid

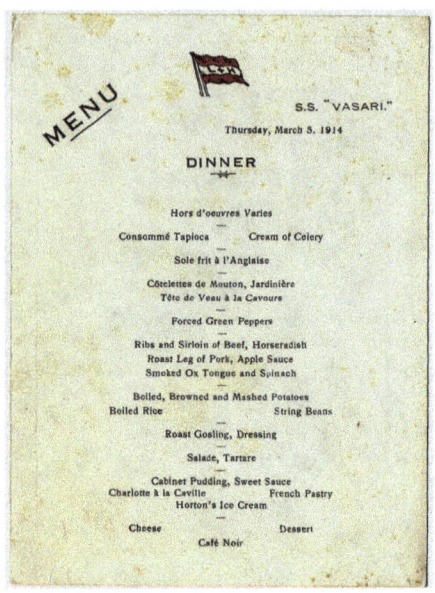

S.S. *Vasari* menu card for Thursday, March 5, 1914.
Author's collection.

The *Vasari* chugged up the east coast of South America with no reports of the troubles of the prior fall's journey from New York. Three days after leaving Rio, the ship stopped in Bahia. A week later, it arrived in the British colony of Trinidad.

Trinidad, the most southern of the Caribbean islands, lies fewer than seven miles off the coast of Venezuela. Green and lush, it provided a respite for everyone. Freed from the steamship's stuffy hold, the horses flipped their manes about in the ocean breeze and toasted their coats in the undiluted sunshine. Show ponies sighed with the weight of riders once again. They cantered into the arena and danced the quadrille with the accuracy and grace of professionals.

Within a few weeks, the SS *Vauban*, another Lamport & Holt v-ship, arrived from Bahia to take the Wild West outfit home. Lulu, along with the other workers, settled in for the final leg of their journey. The turquoise Caribbean lost its sparkle as the gray Atlantic stepped in. The days at sea passed with gossip, food, recollections, and plans. Everyone had plans.

"Verandah Café." S.S. *Vauban*. Postcard. Author's collection.

On the tenth of April, the *Vauban's* passengers crawled into bed. They expected to leave their elegant steel prison the next day. Soon, they would reclaim their land legs and freedom. They would choose when and what to eat, who to sit beside at breakfast — when, and even if, to bathe. Their five-month South American adventure was ending.

"First Class smoke room." S.S. *Vauban*. Postcard. Author's collection.

Lulu and her traveling companions slumbered in the attractive saloon quarters of the luxury liner, as fancy — and almost as comfortable — as a fine hotel. Less fortunate passengers bunked in its windowless bowels. At least one of these steerage class passengers did not sleep much, if at all.

In the blackest heart of the night, the *Vauban* drew even with Sandy Hook, New Jersey. Fewer than twenty miles ahead, Manhattan and her sister boroughs rose from the ocean. According to that day's *New York Evening World*, Syrian immigrant Abram Sabah left his berth to rummage about in Hold No. 2. A mishmash of the show people's trunks, lariats, costumes, souvenirs, and props were piled there, ready to be unloaded. Maybe he was curious, or broke, or simply an incurable thief. Whatever drove him, like Pandora, he settled on a box and opened it. Darkness obscured its contents, so Sabah lit a match to see better. The box held sharpshooter cartridges, all loaded with shot, ready to blast glass target balls lobbed in the air. The match fell from his hand.

Within seconds, all dreams on the *Vauban* crashed to a halt. As if the devil were popping corn in Hell, a series of staccato explosions boomed out of Hold No. 2. Sabah's clothing caught fire. He raced screaming through steerage. As he ran, he ripped his burning clothing off, setting a string of small fires in the other passengers' bedding. Pandemonium followed in his wake.

Edith Tantlinger later recalled the trip:

> *I remember the time our boat the SS Vauban, carrying hundreds of head of cattle, with the Indians and cowboys, caught fire mid-ocean. Women in hysterics buckled life preservers around them and had to be restrained from leaping in the sea. But cowgirls have steel nerves. I was proud of the way our people showed their mettle.*

Beatrice Brosseau, with more bravery than sense, rushed downstairs and through the smoke-filled steerage section. She reached her black stallion, given to her in Trinidad, and was able to pat him and call his name before she was whisked away to safety. She then turned her attention to the steerage passengers and worked to quiet them. Jane Fuller occupied herself with the panicked passengers who were vying for the lifeboats.

The *Vauban* managed to make it to its Brooklyn dock that day, April 11, with no loss of life. Sabah was hauled away to the hospital at Ellis Island, a likely deportee as soon as his burns healed. Before the day was done, an investigation was completed, and its details were published in the newspaper.

Despite the chaos of the near-disaster, immigration officials did their duty and diligently recorded the standard information for arrivals to the States. Lulu, slashing off a decade, told the officials she was thirty years old. For her home address, she claimed a five-story brick apartment building on Manhattan's Upper East Side. The newish building sported carved wreaths, fruit festoons, and Greenman grotesques with roaring mouths on its first-floor brownstone facade. Park Avenue was a block and a half away, and the Metropolitan Museum of Art, three blocks. Who paid the rent on this fine living space, who lived in it, and whether Lulu ever set foot in it are all matters of conjecture.

Hovering in the background was another, eviler, explanation of the fire on the SS *Vauban*. War was brewing in the spring of 1914. World War I — the Great War, the War to End All Wars — would ignite less than four months after the explosions on the *Vauban*. Forces were shoving each other around, jockeying for position before things officially began. Significant clandestine activity was well underway.

South African Fritz Joubert Duquesne was a top-notch spy. His forty-year espionage career began during the Boer War when he spied against the British. In 1914, the handsome fraud began spying for the Germans. With a fake name and under the cover of being a rubber plant researcher, he was sent to Bahia, Brazil. From there, he began sinking British merchant ships. Duquesne's technique was to disguise bombs as mineral samples and time them to explode when the ships were out to sea. He was eventually credited with sinking twenty-two ships in this way and nearly sinking another. He was also credited with starting a fire on the SS *Vauban*.

"Capt. Fritz Duquesne." Courtesy of Library of Congress.

It is not clear if the *Vauban* fire attributed to Duquesne occurred on April 11, 1914, or a different date. The media covered no other fire on the *Vauban*. In 1918, newspapers reported an attempt that year to sink another ship bound from South America to New York. The article noted the men responsible for this effort, *received money from Germany "for services rendered," and that they have been engaged in a long career of spurlos ersenkt ("sink without a trace") wickedness in South America...Since their operations in South America the ss. Salvador was completely destroyed by fire, the ss. Vauban was barely saved from complete destruction by the same cause...*

A British paper tied Duquesne and the *Vauban* together in 1919. It alluded to the "veil of secrecy behind which the Special Service works," to counter foreign espionage. It published a "List of Outrages" perpetuated by Duquesne including "S.S. *Vauban* barely escaped complete destruction."

Whether the explosions stemmed from Abram Sabrah poking around in the hold or from a Duquesne bomb, the SS *Vauban's* passengers — Lulu included — had evaded catastrophe for another day.

Lulu was returning to the States without her latest husband, smooth-faced Charley Mulhall, but she was not alone. Along with her roan show pony, she'd have her new pet marmoset. The tiny monkey, small enough to pose standing on the barrel of a revolver, was — in Lulu's words, "cute." Spring in the city was erupting around her, though she'd not stick around to enjoy it. Soon, very soon, she'd be on the move again.

BE BRAVE AND GO
LIKE A MAN

*On the Road in the United States
Spring 1914*

Almost the minute their pointy-toed boots touched American soil, the Wild West troupe hit the trail. The Tantlingers and Beatrice Brosseau stuck with Ed Arlington and the Miller brothers. 101 Ranch Wild West was opening at Madison Square Garden in ten days.

Lulu, however, veered off in a new direction — the circus. In May, she joined up with Oklahoma Bill's Wild West show, part of Mighty Washburn's Midway Shows circus. In June, she went with the Barnum and Bailey Circus. By August, Barnum and Bailey Circus was in Wyoming and headed for Vancouver, British Columbia. The klieg light on Lulu's career was narrowing its field. No longer was she an act in a Wild West show. Instead, the Wild West show was becoming a circus act, and she was devolving into a bit player. She wasn't alone in her jump to the circus world. Buffalo Bill spent that summer with the Sells-Floto Circus, an outcome of the foolish business deal that had shouldered the Two Bills show into bankruptcy.

Lulu Bell Parr's blue beaded costume vest. Courtesy of the National Cowgirl Museum and Hall of Fame, Fort Worth, Texas.

Pressure from the burgeoning film industry made the survival of stand-alone Wild West shows less and less feasible. Some fell apart on tour. In July, the manager of the Young Buffalo Bill's Wild West show disappeared. Two hundred and seventy-five performers found themselves stranded in East Alton, Missouri. Initially, they survived on a diet of the food intended for their audience — hot dogs, hamburgers, and peanuts. This quickly ran out. Local churches and the county government were called in to help. Similar fates destroyed other shows. Those that survived, except for the 101 Ranch show, had shriveled in size and impact to become small add-ons to circuses. Typically, these Wild West displays came at the end of the traditional circus presentation. At times, they were only ten minutes' worth of entertainment.

Lulu was hitting her own bumps in the road. On August

12, 1914, she wrote a letter. Lulu's education had stopped at third grade, but she learned enough to vividly share her story with twenty-two-year-old cousin Ralph Bolitho. Ralph lived with his parents back in Cadiz Junction, Ohio. He had been taking care of her show pony Taffy for several years, the tough pinto who carried Lulu from Philadelphia to Cadiz Junction back in 1908.

> *My Dear Ralph,*
> *Just a few lines to let you know I am still alive, but came near be sent home to you already for burial — last Fri afternoon my Bucking horse was – bucking down the line fine his head between his knees I had taken off my big black Mexican hat and hit him over the ears, looked up at the crowd with a broad smile the horse slipped and turned a complete sumersalt over me I doubled up in a ball and went under him for he went so quick I had no chance to jump. Broke my arm Cut my eye – doctor took 2 stitches in it – hurt the top of my skull bruised and there is no feeling on one side of my head my back cracked as he went over me and I thought it was broke – he rolled over I rolled away for fear he would fall back on me I jumped up ran out with blood flowing down my face Doctor sewed me face up splintered my arm or done it up in boards or splints and bandages and I am wearing big smoked glasses to protect the sight now and cover up those big bruised eyes I am a sight but glad I came out so lucky.*

After sending her love to all, Lulu added a postscript:

Hope the time will soon fly away and I will see you again soon. I will soon be all right again and I get my money every week.
Well you never go till God calls you then be brave and go like a man. The little monkey is beside while I write and cute as ever.

Lulu's reunion with her young cousin was not to be. Two weeks after she wrote him, Ralph spent a Saturday at a party with friends and came home after dark. He took a flashlight, fetched Taffy, and led him to his nighttime field which was across the Panhandle Railroad tracks. As he headed home in the dark, a train hit and gravely injured Ralph. Taken to the hospital in Steubenville, he died the next day.

Lulu was too injured by the mishap she'd described to Ralph to work. Annie Oakley and Lulu had corresponded as early as 1908. Annie, aware of Lulu's injuries sent her an ornately decorated ivory-handled gun, engraved "To Lulu from Annie – Get Well Soon – 1914."

Lulu's husband, Charley Mulhall, was not as gracious. With few options, she turned to her estranged husband and met with him. His ever-involved father, Zack, tagged along, most likely to keep the reins on his brash son. It's doubtful a reignition of the pair's passion fit with Zack's plans for Charley. The men refused to help her and suggested she get a divorce.

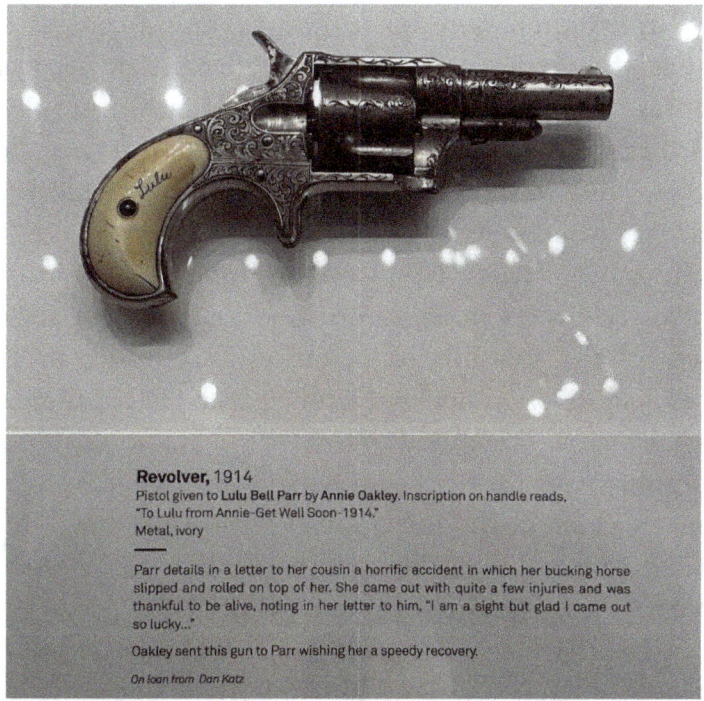

Lulu Bell Parr's gun gifted to her by Annie Oakley in 1914. On permanent display at the National Cowgirl Museum and Hall of Fame. Photography courtesy of the National Cowgirl Museum and Hall of Fame, Fort Worth, Texas.

Though her father was a faint ghost of a parent, Lulu kept in touch with the Parr side of her family. They often came through with friendship, lodging, and help. In October, Lulu turned to her uncle Caleb Parr and stayed with him for several weeks. A tobacconist by trade, Caleb made his living making and selling cigars and other products. After the Civil War, he and his wife had gradually made their way west from Allegheny County, Pennsylvania. His wife birthed children in one small town after another until they reached Peirce City, Missouri. There, they settled down and the last two of the eight Parr children were born. Five of Lulu's cousins lived nearby at the time of her visit and were close to her in age. There was time and opportunity for warm family hospitality.

On Halloween, Lulu left Peirce City for her home in Cadiz Junction, Ohio, and a mournful reunion with Ralph's parents.

She had business to do. On November 23, her attorney filed divorce papers in St. Louis. She asked for an absolute divorce on the grounds of desertion. According to Lulu, Charley had deserted her on October 28th, 1913, three days after their marriage; refused to live with her; and promised to find employment for her in his half-sister Lucille's vaudeville troupe — which he did not do. Her attorney claimed he had no idea where Lulu was living. Charley did not contest the divorce and it was granted February 23, 1915.

Later in 1915, over a four-day Fourth of July round-up in Billings, Montana, Charley Mulhall became enchanted with the elected queen of the round-up, Iva Parks. A week after the rodeo ended, Charley eloped with Ivy.

Lulu, now twice divorced, soldiered on. In May 1915, she was living in Cadiz Junction, Ohio. She wrote a letter asking to compete in the upcoming World Champion Bucking Contest at Frontier Days in Prescott, Arizona. She was advised that there were no purses for lady bucking horse riders, but she was free to compete against the men. There's no documentation that she took them up on the offer. How Lulu spent the remaining months of 1915 is unknown. Whether she left the country to tour again or stayed stateside, bets are good she stayed in the saddle.

THE TRIED-AND-TRUE BLUE

Pittsburgh
July 1916

By July 1916, Lulu was riding for her original mentor, Pawnee Bill. Even-keeled Pawnee Bill lacked Buffalo Bill's personal magnetism, but he was steady, solid, sensible. Maybe he wasn't a tall galoot on a white horse like his old mentor Buffalo Bill, but he was trustworthy. He had been making movies of his Wild West show after the 1913 implosion of the Two Bills. In July, a pared-down Pawnee Bill's Wild West show opened for a six-week run in a Pittsburgh amusement center, Kennywood Park. Princess Wenona and twenty-three Native Americans were among the seventy-five performers. Sixty horses, four mules, and a couple of ponies handled the four-legged work — pint-sized when compared with Pawnee Bill's earlier extravaganzas.

A woman reporter visited the show grounds and was treated to a sit-down dinner with Pawnee Bill. The main course was jerked buffalo meat from one of his bison. Reconstituted with water, rolled in breadcrumbs, then cooked, the meat was "mighty good" according to the diplomatic reporter. She spent...

…one of the most interesting afternoons I ever had known. There is Lulu Parr, who thinks life is tame unless she is astride a horse, giving an imitation of the Frick building, or one of a small boat in a choppy sea. She is a champion rider of bucking bronchos and how she manages to stick on the backs of those bits of chain lightning is a puzzle…Miss Parr lavishes her affection on a little marmoset.

From there, Pawnee Bill's show moved on to the Hardin County Fair at Kenton, Ohio. The Wild West show no longer charged admission. Anyone who paid the twenty-five cents admission to the fair was free to enjoy the Wild West show.

Diane Helentjaris

Newspaper clippings from August 1916. Courtesy of Scott Suther.

Pawnee Bill's former partner and mentor Buffalo Bill had finally extricated himself from his contract with the Sells-Floto circus but could not afford his own Wild West show. He joined up with the Miller brothers to create the "Buffalo Bill (Himself) and the 101 Ranch Wild West Combined, with the Military Pageant [of] Preparedness" show, also known as the 101 Ranch and Buffalo Bill Wild

West show. World War I was well underway in Europe and the show endeavored to tap into Americans' nervousness over their own country's fitness for self-preservation. The show included military routines juxtapositioned with the standard roping, shooting, and riding. However, Chicago's large German-American population was likely to find the theme redolent of anti-German sentiment. A quick name change was in order. The show was advertised in Chicago as the "Chicago Shan-Kive and Round-Up." *Shan-kive* was touted as a Ute Native American word meaning "celebration." Held at the old Cubs' West Side Ball Park for nine days in August, Native Americans, Siberian Cossacks, Bedouins, Japanese, and Mexican vaqueros performed twice daily. Cowboys and cowgirls competed for prize money.

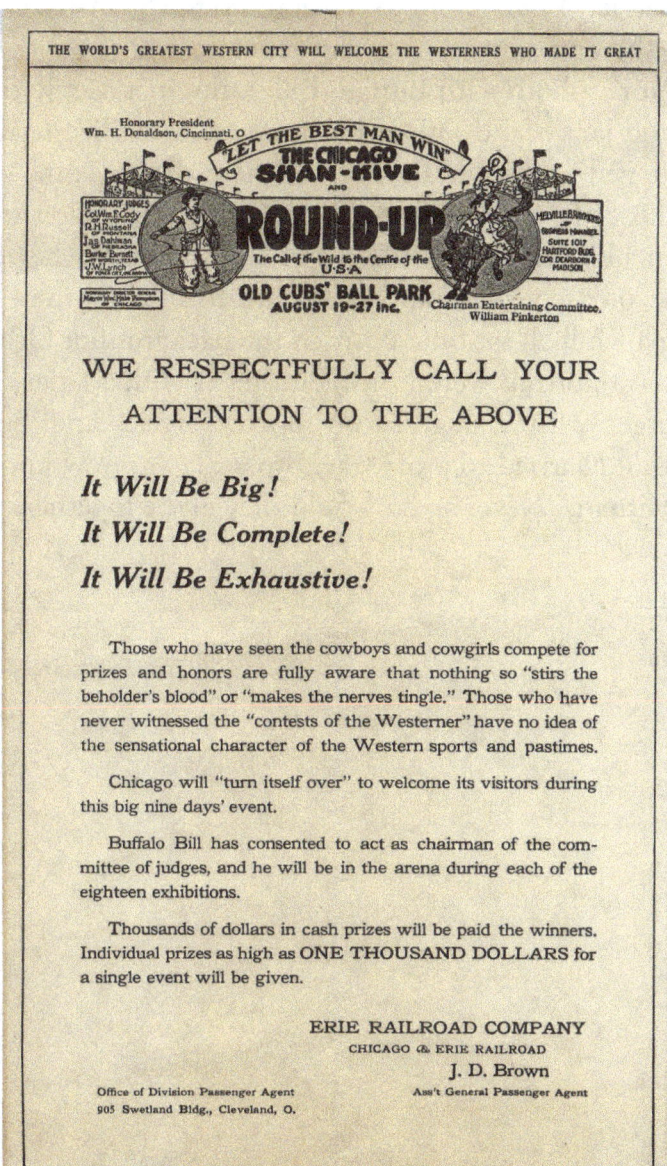

The Chicago Shan-Kive and Round-Up – Broadside. 1916. Object ID# 2019.4.2, Buffalo Bill Museum and Grave, Golden, Colorado.

I Ain't Afraid

Lulu left Pawnee Bill to travel up to the Shan-Kive. Once there, she and nine of the country's most talented cowgirls posed for a photo with Buffalo Bill. Lulu, in a deeply fringed skirt and jacket and one of her trademark big Western hats, sat snugged up to Buffalo Bill but there was no smile on her face. Directly behind Buffalo Bill, Lulu's former sister-in-law Lucille Mulhall leaned forward and draped her hands on the old scout's shoulders. Lulu's former mother-in-law Georgia Mulhall sat on a pony in the background. Others in the group portrait were Edith Tantlinger with a lariat, Bessie Herberger with a dog, Fanny Sperry Steele, and Beatrice Brosseau. Married to a cowboy, Brosseau was now known as "Bea Kirnan." Never again would they all be together.

William F. "Buffalo Bill" Cody and Cowgirls from the 101 Ranch Wild West at the Chicago Shan-Kive. Back Row (left to right) Fanny Sperry Steele, unknown, Beatrice Brosseau Kirnan, Lucille Mulhall, unknown, Edith Tantlinger. Front Row (left to right) Bessie Herberg, unknown, Buffalo Bill, Lulu Bell Parr. Georgie Mulhall (Mary Smith) is believed to be the woman on the horse. Buffalo Bill Center of the West, Cody, Wyoming, USA. (wfc.img.pho.p.69.854 Buffalo Bill Online Archive MS6 Wm. F. Cody Collection)

Not shy of shifting from one show to another, after the Shan-Kive, Lulu joined up with Buffalo Bill. The 101 Ranch and Buffalo Bill Wild West show headed out one evening from Lexington, deep in Virginia's Shenandoah Valley. Their destination was Norfolk on the Chesapeake Bay, over two hundred miles to the east. Scheduled to arrive at seven in the morning, the show would unload in time for a morning parade through town.

To get there, their railroad cars traveled by steam locomotive on the Virginian Railroad. The line connected the Appalachian coal fields with coastal shipping ports. Nicknamed "the Richest Little Railroad in the World" for its commitment to quality equipment, its fleet of steam engines were state-of-the-art. Like beasts after prey, they attacked Virginia's mountains, curves, steep grades, tunnels, and flatlands, rolling them under their wheels.

Engine No. 428 pulled out of Roanoke at midnight with the Wild West show on board and headed up out of the Shenandoah Valley. The locomotive aimed for the spine of the Blue Ridge Mountains. Behind trailed twenty-five cars — five passenger cars, six stock cars, and fourteen flat cars. Four hundred show people were on board.

In the Sunday morning darkness of October 7th, the train was up and over the mountains. Near the coastal Tidewater region of Virginia, Engine No. 428 lurched at 4:30 AM and derailed. With it, toppled several livestock cars. Explanations for the derailment included excess speed, a broken stock car axle, and a switch malfunction. The show people claimed an open switch caused the wreck. The railroad denied this. Others blamed a mismatch between the antiquated circus cars and the powerful modern equipment. No one was happy with the outcome.

Thirty-one horses died, some outright and others by euthanasia. About the same number were injured. One person was hurt when an injured horse kicked them.

Eleven of the destroyed horses had been trained arena

mounts. "Among the killed horses was the one belonging to Miss Lola [Lulu] Parr and greatly prized by her. It was imported from South America." The little roan pony Hank Gibbons gave Lulu in South America was dead. As *The Virginian-Pilot* reported,

> *Many of the performers were completely 'broken up' yesterday. Horses that they had been riding, that they had known for years and loved as if they were human beings, will never lift their heads and prick up their ears to the sound of a bugle call, nor stamp impatiently as they wait for the shrill blast of the arena director's whistle to send them galloping wildly before an enthusiastic audience. The other horses, too, knew that something was wrong. Not for hours after they reached the grounds yesterday morning did they regain their composure. Many of the riders yesterday had to go through their stunts on unaccustomed horses and many of the horses had to do double duty. But the audience would never have known there was a thing in the world to disturb the equilibrium of that perfect organization that is represented by almost any big show.*

The show managed to scrape together a parade and two shows on Monday. The plan was for them to tour a bit in the region, and then return to Norfolk for the winter. Ads in the local paper asked for farmers with pasturage for their horses. The Hotel Monticello housed Ed Arlington and others.

Buffalo Bill's last public appearance was in Portsmouth, across the Elizabeth River from Norfolk, on November 11,

1916. It was the closing act for one of America's greatest showmen. His covey of cowgirls flocked to the white-haired gentleman's tent after the show for a final drink from his silver punchbowl — a gift from Queen Victoria — and a goodbye kiss. Lulu, unable or unwilling to face the sorrowful scene, refused to join them. The next day Buffalo Bill teased her. She later recalled to a reporter,

> *"I don't believe in saying good-bye, Colonel," she told him. "Let's just make it 'Au revoir.' "Buffalo Bill agreed and extended his hand. "Au revoir," he said, "and don't you dare sign up with any other show. I'll see you next spring."*

Buffalo Bill died on January 10, 1917, in Denver, Colorado. The world wept.

THE COWBOY BOXER

Oklahoma
1916

By the end of 1916, Joe Miller recognized the war clouds looming on the horizon for what they were. He believed, as had always been the case, that the coming conflagration promised more profit for suppliers than entertainers. He sold the 101 Ranch Wild West livestock and equipment to his partner Ed Arlington. Miller planned to concentrate his business skills on raising meat, livestock, and food back on the 101 Ranch in Oklahoma.

Arlington rented the deceased Buffalo Bill's name. Combining the classic moniker with his newly-purchased, used equipment, he minted a "new" Buffalo Bill Wild West show in 1917.

Things did not go well. Bad weather kept attendance down. Pre-war measures cramped transportation and resources. Arlington sold the show midseason to an unlikely successor — Jess Willard, the reigning world heavyweight champion.

I Ain't Afraid

Jess Willard. 1915. Courtesy of Library of Congress.

Willard was a gargantuan man. Few men had his stature of six feet and six-and-a-half inches in height. Few had arms with his eighty-three-inch reach or "wingspan." Boxing against Willard was rarely a fair fight.

He was also, in the racist parlance of the times, the Great White Hope — the man who had defeated Jack Johnson, the first African American to gain the heavyweight title. Their title fight in Havana, Cuba had been a grueling set-to in 1915. Willard ended it with a 26th-round knock-out.

Truth be told, Willard did not particularly enjoy boxing. For him, it was a way to tap into his physicality and feed his wife and five children. What he did like was horses. Referred to as "the cowboy boxer," he grew up on a farm in Kansas and early on, recognized his gift in dealing with horseflesh. He trained, swapped, and shoed horses until tumbling into boxing.

Once he gained the world champion heavyweight title, Willard did little to defend it. Instead, he indulged his first love and became a Wild Wester. In 1915, he partnered with the Miller brothers as a side attraction with their 101 Ranch Wild West; the next year, he was with the Sells-Floto circus. He rode horses in the Grand Entrance parades, decked out in a cowpuncher hat and boots. People flocked to see the man who had bested Jack Johnson. He gave boxing exhibitions but also riding ones. Money rolled in.

Lulu, already with the new Buffalo Bill show, stayed on as a headliner for the "Buffalo Bill and Wild West Show with Jess Willard." She earned flattering media attention such as printed by the *Nashville Banner*:

> *Miss Stickney [bareback equestrienne with the circus] in her riding illustrates the modern circus method of high-class equestrianism. Lula Parr, another chic and attractive young woman, is the antithesis of Miss Stickney as a rider. There is nothing of the dainty posing of the circus in her horsemanship. Her riding is of the wild, reckless, devil-may-care kind that thrills the blood and makes one involuntarily wonder how so frail an appearing young woman could put so much abandon in her handling of wild horses. It is said there is no "outlaw" pony in the entire Jess Willard Buffalo Bill stable that Miss Parr cannot ride. She is the "stormy petrel" of the arena.*

I Ain't Afraid

Two months earlier, in Denver, another female bronco rider, Maggie Wright, died of head injuries at age twenty, two hours after her mount somersaulted over a fence. She had initially declined to ride the horse — named Gentle Annie — till taunts from the cowboys changed her mind. Her dying words were said to be, "Well, I rode her." She had been riding before a crowd of hundreds as part of a motion picture filming event. Beatrice Brosseau and Lulu, working for Jesse Willard that summer, rode upside down, bareback, and without a bridle. Like gladiators entertaining Romans, Willard's cowboys and cowgirls gave…

> *a "punch" to the performance that is peculiarly western, and the very danger of injury or worse that they dare injects a thrill into the performance not to be obtained in any other way.*

THE OPTIMISTIC HEART

Washington, DC
November 1917

Wartime drives many to the altar. Maybe it was understandable that Orth Barcus, USN sought matrimony. The United States had declared war on Germany in April 1917. Barcus signed up for the Navy in July and was initially sent to Norfolk, Virginia. By November, when the war was in full swing, he decided to marry.

But how the twenty-two-year-old sailor landed on forty-one-year-old Lulu as his choice, beyond her obvious beauty and charm, is lost in the mists of time, the fog of war, the haze of hormones. Perhaps it was the Indiana connection. Orth grew up about 120 miles from Lulu's Fort Wayne birthplace. His family was rooted in the northeast section of Indiana. His father George owned a series of businesses and did well. As if to emphasize her Indiana connection, Lulu gave Fort Wayne as her home when the two applied for their marriage license in Washington, DC. The *Indianapolis Sunday Star* confirmed the marriage occurred in its section "News of Hoosier Folk."

Orth was no cowboy. Tall, black-haired, and brown-eyed, Orth had been employed as a tool maker at the Warren Gear Company in Muncie, Indiana before joining the US Navy.

I Ain't Afraid

He had also been married before.

In December 1912, Orth and his girlfriend, both Wabash High School students, had traveled up to a village in Michigan one morning, married using distortions of their real names, went back home, and kept their marriage secret for two months. When news of the marriage broke, the town paper characterized them both as "estimable young people," yet snickered that not even their parents had known they were wed. In May, shortly after the couple moved into a furnished home, seventeen-year-old Orth left "for parts unknown." His father claimed to have no idea where the youngster was. His teenage wife sued and won a divorce on the grounds of cruel and "inhuman" treatment.

After her marriage to Orth, Lulu continued with her career. Orth was, at least part of the time, presumably at sea. She opened with Ringling Brothers, Barnum and Bailey Circus in March 1920 at Madison Square Garden. "The Circus Colossal" boasted "elephants and more elephants until it seemed as if the great arena would be over-run with elephants." Beyond the roller-skating bears, "educated" pigs, boxing kangaroos, clowns, and acrobats there was a mere ten minutes of the "wildest Wild West."

The band of cowboys and cowgirls included at least two cowboys Lulu had previously worked with — Cy Compton and Hank Durnell. Durnell was the poor wretch who, when sick with smallpox, had begged to be thrown overboard from the S.S. *Vasari*. At the Madison Square Garden gig, Lulu once again was injured. She fractured some ribs which, along other injuries, kept her out of the show for two months. Undaunted, after she recuperated, she rejoined the troupe to forge on with her job.

On September 27, Orth's mother, Ruby, wrote to Lulu.

Ruby Barcus was an educated woman, having attended the University of Kansas. Her literacy was on display in the letter along with her questionable sensitivity. Penned on industrial stationery emblazoned with the heading "Rock City Manufacturing Co., Manufacturers of The Wabash Magnetizer," it said,

> *Dear Lulu.*
> *Rec'd your card this A.M. I ans. Your letter the 19th the day after I recd yours & sent it to the return address you had on envelop as it was too late to reach you where you said you would be on Tues? You may receive it yet. I told you in that letter we were very sorry indeed that you and Orth could not live happily together & it grieved us more than we can tell to know you were divorced but perhaps it is for the best. Glad you are happy in your work. Thank you for the pictures. You look so well. You always enjoyed your profession. Owing to all the circumstances presume it would be best for us not to correspond anymore. You surely have my prayers and sympathy.*
> *Yours very truly,*
> *Mrs. Geo Barcus*

Lulu wrote back from Dayton, Ohio:

> *Dear Mother*
> *Your short letter in Answer to my Card received did not get the letter of which you speak – I did not know Orth got a divorce from me I have never received any notification thereto.*

I Ain't Afraid

I am indeed sorry too for I loved Orth but if he has secured a divorce and don't care to live with me of Course I would not force – him to live with me against [his] will never the less I love him as well and ever more now but would like to have Divorce notification of the Divorce and on what grounds I am sued and I will never trouble you again with any Correspondence I never got a divorce and I never will only in the Show I took Lulu B Parr show name
Yours Truly
Lulu B Parr
Dayton Ohio General Delivery
Pray for me Mother

Fitted into the upper corner of the letter, written upside down, was a final addendum from Lulu:

Orth left me and said he was going to Sea never had much trouble and if you had been near us we would never have had a separation.

Orth had been discharged from the Navy on August 28, 1919 — more than a year earlier. Maybe he signed up for the Merchant Marines or took a job on an ocean liner. Whatever the case, Orth Barcus was gone from his wife Lulu to parts unknown. Again.

Lulu finished the Wild West season in Nashville on the 27th of October 1920. In January 1921, she stopped in Ashland, Ohio to visit her uncle George Sheehan before heading off to join a vaudeville act. Interviewed while in Ohio, she shared,

...Out at Los Angeles when some friends and I were going past a church we saw a bride all in white come out with the bridegroom. "Lulu," said one of the girls, "do you reckon you'll ever look like that? Why don't you quit the show business and get married?"

"I've tamed some of the fiercest bronchos going," said I, but I draw the line on trying to tame a man. I'm not going to take any chances with a husband until I've saved enough money to be independent."

TIME FOR TIGER SKIN AND THE TANTLINGERS

On the Road in the United States
1921

Lulu either couldn't or wouldn't or, at least, didn't veer from her chosen life as a Wild West performer. All the large Wild West shows evaporated by 1918, wafted away like smoke from a campfire — Buffalo Bill was dead, Jess Willard's Wild West folded after one year, Pawnee Bill and the Miller Brothers were sticking close to their ranches. Not only had the film industry nibbled incessantly at their heels and siphoned off the public's entertainment budget, but World War I had gobbled up men and horses. It was more difficult to hire Native Americans. New government officials at the Lakota reservations frowned on performance as a career path for their Native American charges. Traipsing around with traveling shows distracted the Native Americans from their new life as farmers or at least the life the federal government wanted them to follow.

In 1921, Lulu found employment with the Tantlingers, her colleagues from the 101 Ranch Wild West show and fellow survivors of the South American tour. They had started their own little Wild West show, a part of the C.A. Wortham Circus. Verne had years of experience managing other men's Wild West shows. Edith never lost her handy school marm skills. Their business became the largest Wild West show still on the road. Lulu stuck with their Tex-Mex Wild West show for the next three years.

Edith and Lulu, who were about the same age, complemented each other in the program. Lulu took the lead as a horsewoman, the bucking horse rider, and Edith was the sharpshooter, the woman who blasted glass balls out of the air. Cowboys, cowgirls, Native Americans, Cossacks, and comedians rounded out the show which, in 1921, included fifty-two people.

Lulu's celebrity continued to rely on the unique combination of her championship status, beauty, horsewomanship, and eye-popping costumes. Lulu "…has a number of striking costumes and offers some spectacular riding." The "one-time lady champion broncho buster of the frontier days in Cheyenne," was photographed in a flashy tiger-skin riding skirt, long-sleeved top, and embellished big hat. The papers crowed it was "probably the most attractive cowgirl suit in the United States," won as first prize in a Frontier Days celebration. Publicity stories often mentioned the gold medal she wore, "emblematic of the honors she won in the saddle, which was presented to her by the late Theodore Roosevelt, one of the judges in Cheyenne, Wyoming."

> *She is attracting attention with her many and varied costumes and her riding of bucking broncs. Miss Parr is considered the best show woman in her line in the United States.*

Lulu Bell Parr's performance clothing on display at the National Cowgirl Museum and Hall of Fame. Courtesy of the National Cowgirl Museum and Hall of Fame, Fort Worth, Texas.

The *Atlanta Constitution*, with a whiff of the backhanded compliment, in 1921 printed that "Miss Parr is riding better today than ever before, and she appears at every performance given in this big attraction." Lulu was edging up to two decades in the public eye and though she could shave years off her stated age, she could not deny the passage of time. Little girls who saw her ride early in her career now had children of their own to bring to the circus.

The passing of time brought wins and losses. For Lulu, with no family of her own, losing a pet was particularly traumatic. In 1921, her pet marmoset was stolen as the circus toured in Butte, Montana. Lulu took the time to share details with a newspaper reporter on the tiny primate's rarity, its earlier bout with pneumonia, and showed a photograph of it posed on the barrel of a gun. She offered a twenty-five-dollar reward for its return. There was no happy reunification story published.

BACK TO BRITAIN AND BEYOND

New York
May 1924

The bugle blared. Adventure called. After three years of touring with the Tantlingers, it was time for something new. Lulu was going back to Europe with London first up on her list.

The British government was pulling together an extravaganza, the British Empire Exhibition, to celebrate — of all things — British colonialism. Never mind the Irish Free State had wrested its liberty a mere two years earlier or that the UK had committed itself to leaving India or that the United States was more than one hundred years into its independence. The powers that be believed the Exhibition would not only stimulate trade, but also strengthen the bonds between Mother Britain and her colonies. The Prince of Wales headed up the committee putting the program together. Later crowned King Edward VIII, he would infamously abdicate his throne to marry American divorcee Wallis Simpson.

Sprawled over two hundred acres on the outskirts of

London, the Exhibition entertained over twenty-seven million visitors during the warmer months of 1924 and 1925. Multiple new buildings and the Empire Stadium, later known as Wembley Stadium, were erected. A refrigerated statue of the Prince of Wales carved from butter was one exhibit as well as his mother's over-the-top doll's house. Other, more scientific, exhibits displayed fabrics, automobiles, and aeronautical advances. Strollers gawked at live exotic animals and in one memorable event, watched a set-to among three bathing elephants. In true tone-deaf style, the Brits displayed live colonists. Nigerians sat in a newly built walled city and demonstrated metalwork and leatherwork. West African students in London complained that these misrepresented their land's current stage of development. Anti-colonial feelings were on the rise. Indian nationalists called for a boycott.

American rodeo promoter Tex Austin believed he recognized an opportunity when he saw it. Known as the "King of the Rodeo" and "Daddy of the Rodeo," Tex did his level best to expand the rodeo market into new settings. He claimed to have produced the first indoor rodeo in 1918 in Wichita, Kansas. He then produced the first "World's Championship Rodeo" at Madison Square Garden. Tex planned, for his next act, to put on the first international rodeo. The role of such a predominantly American event at a colonial exhibition was sidestepped with plans to include participants from Canada and Australia. Austin pulled together over two hundred performers for his "First International Rodeo or Cowboy Championships."

Tex Austin was a large man making large plans. The *Santa Fe New Mexican* described him as "a great big chap – considerably over six feet tall, straight as an arrow, and of striking appearance," wearing a solid gold steer's-head stickpin "the size of a twenty-dollar gold piece." What he wasn't was a Texan or even an Austin, though he kept his true origins to himself. He claimed to be from west Texas. Others said he was born Clarence Von Norstrand in Missouri, specifically St. Louis. Years later, the *New York Times* would declare him to be a Jewish man from North Carolina who had gone west. His tales of fighting in the Mexican Revolution as a Captain (or *capitano*) under Pancho Villa may have been exaggerated.

"Tex Austin, of Las Vegas, New Mex., calls on Pres. Coolidge to ask the good offices of the Amer. fov't officials in London for the 100 Amer. cowboys and cowgirls who go to the Brit. Empire exposition to compete in the championship contests in the Imperial Stadium for the

Diane Helentjaris

International championship titles, Trophies, and $75,000 in purses. Tex Austin will manage the contest [White House, Washington, D.C.]" 1924. Photograph by Harris & Ewing. Courtesy of Library of Congress.

For Lulu, the Intercolonial Rodeo in London beckoned as a boost to her career, an event to bolster her publicity, a source of new bragging rights. To gain these benefits, she settled into the role of being one in a crowd of cowboys, cowgirls, Native Americans, buffaloes, steers, and horses. At heart, Lulu was a performer, an accomplished horsewoman, more than she was a rodeo competitor. Things played out as expected. Lulu was overlooked in the printed program. Instead, the publicity emphasized the younger crowd of cowgirls, those still cutting their teeth (and breaking their ribs), roping, and riding. Few of the women were mentioned by name and fewer still were included in publicity photos, charming as they were. Testosterone ruled the day for this rodeo.

The ocean liner SS *Menominee* pulled out of New York on May 22, 1924, with its load of cowboys and cowgirls. On board was a gift for the Prince of Wales, a "spirited eight-year-old mustang" named Tejana who could "stop on a dime, turn on a nickel, and throw a steer at one toss." Newspapers described the Prince of Wales as "positively the world's worst rider," so this may not have been the most sensitive gift. His Highness's tumbles and fractures were routinely covered in the newspapers with mean-spirited reporters keeping a running tally of his falls. Yet, in a display of royal manners, the prince let it be known he was "very much pleased with the 'hoss' and appreciates the generosity of his American cowboy friend."

The trip across the Atlantic was, unfortunately, not a pacific one. On board, a special correspondent for *The London*

Daily Express shared,

> *Pitiable scenes were witnessed yesterday. The white-faced champions lay rigid in deck chairs, muffled in rugs and blankets. Low groans broke the deathly silence. The heavy swells and pouring rains had conquered the redoubtable riders. Many have expressed the determination to settle in England in preference to the return voyage.*

Lassoing was prominent on this tour. Canadian champion cowboy Peter Vandermeer

> *…produced a lasso at lunch today and provided the passengers with a vivid display of lasso skill. He roped the rolls, knives, forks, and serviettes. An officer carrying meat to his mouth on a fork found the food suddenly snatched from his grasp… His final feat was the lassoing of a single pea.*

The cowgirls, in their non-conformist manner, garnered a different type of attention.

> *Cowgirls' fashions would drive a dress designer to despair…The girls, who are all beautiful, wear weird and costly clothes. One appeared at lunch in a pink silk boudoir cap. Most cowgirls appear at breakfast wearing afternoon hats and sleeveless frocks. All wear immense diamond and platinum rings.*
>
> *The indulgent cowboy husbands, wearing rags themselves, insist on their wives appearing at all*

times in full finery. There is a strange contrast in the outfits of the husbands and wives. The cowgirls rouge to excess, while the husbands are unshaven.

The Menominee is now an exact replica of a Wild West saloon or a floating ranch. The cowboys sprawl on the floor laying dice. The wives dance to the gramophone or piano.

The SS *Menominee's* arrival in Britain was captured in a *British Pathè* news short. One hundred and thirty "Cowboys and girls" along with 240 broncos arrived in England on June 6. One-hundred-and-sixty-nine wild steers had arrived two days earlier. One cowboy stood high above the deck, balancing his pointy-toed boots on a rope ladder, and swinging his hat. Others twirled lariats, danced in and out of the circling ropes, and lassoed the cameraman. Cowgirls in floppy scarves and huge hats smiled for the film. Other shorts featured cowboy Skeeter Bill Robbins studying to be an English "Dude" with a big cigar jammed in his mouth and wearing a monocle.

The exuberance and extroverted behavior continued throughout the tour, not always to good effect. Buffalo Bill had paved the way in Britain with multiple tours of his Wild West show, but Tex Austin was breaking new ground bringing a rodeo to the United Kingdom. The British had never been exposed to the rough realities of life as practiced by American cattlemen. Cotswold cattle slowly ambled in bucolic hedgerowed fields. They did not plod hundreds of dusty miles of American grassland to reach clanging and rumbling railroad yards. English cattle were not chased by yipping roughneck cowboys swinging lariats. No, they were not. Brits had never seen the like of Yankee animal husbandry.

I Ain't Afraid

Program for Austin's "First International Rodeo or Cowboy Championships" held in Wembly. Author's collection.

On June 14, opening day for the rodeo, a steer's leg was broken as it was roped. Many in the audience of 130,000 rose to their feet, hissed, and booed. Some walked out. Officials of the Royal Society for the Prevention of Cruelty to Animals threatened to bring the matter before Parliament. The roping contests continued "privately" thereafter "in justice to the 80 cowboys who have traveled more than 5000 miles to enter the contests." Breakaway loops were used in roping and bulldoggers were limited to "marking" the steers with their hands as they rode by. But the activists for the humane treatment to animals were not satisfied. Eventually, the Home Secretary ordered the private roping and bulldogging events also stopped and sent 150 police to make sure they were.

On the first night in Britain, a group from Austin's troupe visited a cabaret. A six-foot four-inch cowboy lassoed soloist Loleta Lambert as she sang her song. The next day, cowboys lassoed pretty girls from their automobile, the porter at the Savoy Hotel, and even the statue of Lord Nelson in Trafalgar Square. Texas's *San Angelo Evening Standard* defensively published an article under the title "Our Wild West Cow-Punchers Too Much for Staid London." It noted that though a cowgirl broke her collarbone, and a cowboy injured his leg competing at the rodeo, the Brits were most concerned with the injured steer. It also noted injuries continued in the private contests with one calf suffering a broken neck and another, a lost horn. "But whatever American cowboys are like, England has found them a little too wild for her."

Part of the rodeo was the opening of competition to all comers. Only one Englishman was able to stick on a "bucker's" back in these competitions. The Australians and Canadians did much better. One Australian had such a good reputation that a ranch owner back home placed a one-thousand-pound bet on him.

By June 24, British lawyers were hashing out the ethics of animal treatment at the American rodeo in a cruelty case against the rodeo promoters. Austin and the cowboy bulldogging the steer were released on condition that the bulldogging be cut out of the program. By July 16, Austin's rodeo outfit had "sailed for home and an international incident is over." The public uproar would be credited with the 1934 passage of British laws to prevent animal cruelty.

One paper noted that the event...

> ...seemed to invest the beefsteak with a disquieting realism. The English are not the only people who prefer to think of their meat products as inanimate in the beginning.

Stereotypes were evoked by both sides. As they headed home, cowboys donned spats, canes, monocles, and sweaters to poke fun at their British cousins.

From London, Austin's group did not go home despite the English press's wishful thinking that they had. Instead, the troupe went on to Dublin to perform at Croke Park. Buffalo Bill had never toured Ireland, so the Irish people's vision of cowboy culture was based on what they saw in the movies and read in books and magazines. Rodeo was fresh to Ireland with few even knowing what a rodeo was. Unlike the British, the Irish for the most part were overwhelmingly positive in their reception thanks to hard work by Austin. He played up his performers' links with the Irish diaspora and strategically supported local charities.

> For us Irish this Rodeo had a special interest if for the names alone. Ruth Roach, Vera McGinnis, Florence Fenton, Bonnie McCarroll, Tommy Kirnan, Mike Hastings, despite spelling, are surely of Irish stock...

Vera McGinnis and Tommy Kirnan became a special focus for the media with their assumed Irish roots. Vera would recall champagne glasses never allowed to be empty. She felt the English crowds seemed hostile. Only in Ireland, she claimed, were she and the rodeo "really appreciated." Whether Lulu's potential Irish ancestry did get mentioned or not is undocumented. Though there were American Parrs who descended from Irish immigrants, most Parrs in the United States were of English or German descent.

Irish men were invited to try their hand at riding broncs, as the English had been. Over thirty-one gave it a try. Most were members of the Free State Army or jockeys. One Irish woman entered the contest but was refused entry as it was "too dangerous for a woman" — never mind all the cowgirl bronco-riders like Lulu who were part of the show.

The rodeo deepened the Irish enchantment with the American West and provoked this poetic response:

> *What excitement down at Croke Park where the Rodeo was staged,*
> *It came to us in Ireland as a boon,*
> *For all the champion riders in the world were engaged,*
> *We had thrills and spills throughout the afternoon…*

After two weeks in Dublin, Tex Austin loaded up his performers to head off to France. It was now September. For ten glorious days, the American rodeo performed before packed audiences at the Buffalo Velodrome near Paris. Business was robust and a portion of the receipts were shared directly with the performers. Specifically, of the two million francs in ticket sales, the group divvied up 250,000 francs — the equivalent at the time of over eleven thousand US dollars. They returned home with souvenirs galore.

I Ain't Afraid

By October 18, Tex Austin was back in New York exhibiting his Champions Rodeo at Madison Square Garden.

In the spring of 1925, Lulu began a run with the Robbins Brothers' 4-ring Circus as part of the attached Ponca Bill Wild West Show. She was a headliner, often the only performer with the Wild West Show to be mentioned by name. She was the "greatest feminine bucking horse rider in the world."

She also appeared, once more, with the newly resurrected Miller Brothers' 101 Ranch Real Wild West:

> *Best dressed of all the cowgirls and girl riders with Miller Brothers' 101 Ranch Real Wild West, coming to Rutland Saturday is Lulu Parr, who has thousands of dollars in beaded frocks, jeweled spurs and saddles…Lulu can ride anything at anytime and anywhere, and she is one of the stars among the three hundred cowboys and cowgirls. She is a great favorite among the Indians for she was adopted by the Crows when she was a tot. They call her 'Morning Sun'…In the world's largest street parade on 101 Ranch Wild West show day, you can pick Lulu out easily. She is a striking and attractive figure.*

Lulu Bell Parr's beaded performance vest with an equine theme. Courtesy of Dan Katz.

Lulu may have not received much press attention in Britain and Europe, but she had gained a new professional experience and did not hesitate to tap it. Newspaper articles proclaimed her as "unquestioned champion horse rider for this country and has won every contest she has entered in Europe and South America…She is the highest salaried wild west rider in the world." Not the highest-paid female Wild West rider, but the highest-paid man or woman. By contract with Robbins, she rode twice a day, on two bucking horses. Her bronco riding was found to be "sensational." She was pushing a half-century in age. What next?

CLOWNING AROUND

Oskaloosa, Iowa
October 31, 1925

To choose a wedding day is to pick an anniversary date. There are couples who pick Valentine's Day, a celebration of hearts and romance, but also one not easily forgotten. Other duos' dates are cramped by expediency — the day the preacher was available or the Saturday when Uncle John was in town. Somehow, someway, Lulu landed on Halloween, 1925, as the best day to marry a clown. What costumes they wore, whether or not she was decked out in her tiger-skin cowgirl outfit, or he slapped on a bulbous red nose and greasepaint was not a matter of record but marry they did. Halloween was officially their anniversary.

The nuptials took place in the washed-up mining town of Newton, Iowa. The groom, Tracy Thomas Andrews, hailed from Oskaloosa, Iowa, about forty miles to the southeast. Grandson of a butcher, son of a farmer, his widowed mother still lived there along with his extended family. However, there is no indication that any of his family attended the ceremony. He claimed his home address as Cincinnati, Ohio — most likely reflecting the use of the entertainment industry's organization *Billboard* to collect his mail. A forthright man, he accurately gave his age as thirty-six and stated this was his first marriage.

Lulu kept to her usual form when dealing with bureaucrats. She lied. She diplomatically gave her age as one less than Tracy's — thirty-five years old — and claimed this marriage to be her first. It was, at least, her fourth. She also claimed her uncle George P. Sheehan's home of Springfield, Illinois as her domicile.

Lulu's newest husband was a strapping fellow — six foot and two inches tall, brown-haired, blue-eyed, with fair skin and big muscles. Few of his Robbins Brothers circus audience would recognize him in civilian clothes. They only knew him either as a tall white-faced clown with a straw hat tipped rakishly to the side or as George Washington in the circus's patriotic pageant. He had finished four years of high school and, unlike many of the cowboys, could write legibly. But mostly Tracy was a clown, a juggling comic clown dedicated to his profession.

Tracy and Lulu shared athleticism and a strong work ethic. Their marriage made it past the three-day mark left by Charley Mulhall, then the one-year mark of Orth Barcus, but puttered out after a year and a half. Tracy stated in his request for a divorce that Lulu had deserted him on April Fool's Day 1927, less than two years after their Halloween wedding.

Lulu had indeed been exploring new opportunities, opportunities which would take her away from Tracy and their shared employer, the Robbins Brothers' circus.

Back East, in Charlotte, Michigan that spring, "Colonel" Emmett D. Snyder was gathering performers for his Wild West show. Known as "Tiger Bill" or "Colonel Snyder," at age eleven, he ran away from his Michigan home to join the Burr Robbins Circus. He had operated his own Wild West show for thirty years. The 1927 season performers were expected to be in Charlotte by May 6 for the opening. They would head up to northern Michigan in a fleet of fifteen motor trucks and wagons.

On April 24, Tiger Bill wrote Lulu from Charlotte, Michigan and perhaps, created an unintended fuss in the Andrews' household. He mailed the letter to her Oskaloosa address. He also called her "Lula" as her family and many of her friends did.

> *Mrs. Lula Parr,*
>
> *Your letter of 18th received note where you say I can depend on you for the season. Now we run a Wild West show using Wild West Canopy. Work out in the open same as all Wild West. We use a few circus acts such as pony drill and so forth between Wild West acts. We put on a concert after the big show where we feature the bucking horse and steer riding.*
>
> *Here is where I am going to feature you. Now, Lula, you certainly think you can earn $35.00 a week or else you wouldn't ask for it now if I didn't think you be worth that much to the show, I would not want you.*
>
> *Now this is a show where everybody gets their pay on pay day – everybody has a contract the same. We run our own cook house and furnish sleeping tents and cots – for our people everybody sleeps on lot, band and performers, everybody the same. Note in regard to your trunks & saddles box they will go in property wagon over road, and you will probably ride in one of the touring cars. Now*

I think I have explained everything so there be no dissatisfaction. Now I will expect you to go in parade ride in tournament. We dance quadrille on horseback. Will just simply make yourself useful in big show same as other girls. Our programs are easy won't overwork you – but your salary must be a secret. Am enclosing a contract. We open here in Charlotte for rehearsal 2 days. Now if everything is OK, please sign contract and return one.
Yours truly,
'E. D. Snyder

P.S. Evidently Lula you been playing rodeo and perhaps been with some shows where you didn't get your pay but here is one show where all you have to do is to help earn it and you get it.

Lulu did not accept Tiger Bill's offer. Newspaper readers in Great Falls, Montana read in May that the Robbins Brother circus, "the largest show in the world giving a street parade" would be in their town on June 9. Among the acts would be "Miss Lulu Parr, world's champion bucking bronco rider. Forty clowns under Kenneth Waite, the world's highest salaried clown…" This tidbit of promotional fairy dust would be sprinkled, word for word, across the Midlands from Chillicothe, Missouri to Chadron, Nebraska for the next four months. Only the date would change.

It wasn't true. Lulu had left the Robbins brothers and all forty-one of their clowns — including her husband Tracy — in the sawdust for the 1927 season. She joined Hagenbeck-Wallace circus and performed in its Cheyenne Bill's Wild West show. With a smile on her face and a huge sombrero on her head, she posed in the front row of Cheyenne Bill's 1927 cast photograph. Her marriage to Tracy Andrews was over.

"Hagenbeck-Wallace Circus featuring Cheyenne Bill's Wild West." 1927. Photograph by Edward J. Kelty. Lulu Bell Parr is in the front seated row, third from left. Billy Rose Theatre Division, The New York Public Library. "Hagenbeck-Wallace Circus featuring Cheyenne Bill's Wild West" New York Public Library Digital Collections. Accessed June 7, 2024.

The *Evening Independent* newspaper carried a story about Lulu in its June 9, 1927, edition which, while it confirmed her work with the Hagenbeck-Wallace circus, raised a question or two… or three. It was such an intriguing story, a Steubenville paper printed a summary of it in their "From Old Files" column fifteen years later.

The original story was erroneously illustrated with a photograph of Hagenbeck-Wallace performer Miss Gene

McDonald on a rearing horse. That wasn't the only mistake. Headlined "Girl Kidnapped by Father 25 Years Ago, Circus Star," it claimed,

> *About 5 years ago the city of Steubenville, Ohio was shocked when news broke out that the father of a little girl had the audacity to come to Steubenville and kidnap his own daughter from her mother, from whom he was separated. In fact, the townsfolk were dumbfounded. Such a thing never before had happened there and great was the consternation.*
>
> *"She'll never amount to much without a mother's training," people were wont to say.*
>
> *No trace was found of the girl, then only 5 years old, and it was not until several years later that Steubenville residents learned that the child was growing into womanhood and "amounting to much," and...in a field unknown to Ohio.*
>
> *The girl is Lulu Parr, woman ex-champion broncho-buster and bucking horse rider, who will be seen with the Hagenbeck-Wallace circus wild west show Saturday afternoon and night...*
>
> *Her father, himself an expert rider gave Lulu a pony. Riding seemed to be born in her and when she was a mere slip of a girl there wasn't a bronk on the ranch she could not subdue. She was "queen of the cowboys" and when any trouble occurred among them it was Lulu who was called in as referee and it was Lulu who settled it amicably to both parties.*

Though the timeline is wrong — Lulu had not been five years old for decades — there may be a grain of truth in this tall tale. Perhaps Lulu's father, William Parr, had taken her out West at some point without her mother Lizzie's permission. The best fibs include a nugget of truth, though mining the ore in Lulu's stories often yielded fool's gold.

When spring came around again, in 1928, Lulu was back with Robbins Brothers' circus. She continued to tout her 1924 participation in Tex Austin's rodeo and gain such publicity as this:

> *She has appeared in most of the foreign countries as a broncho busting cowgirl rider. Only recently she appeared at the Inter-colonial Empire Exposition before the Prince of Wales. Later she appeared in the American Rodeo at Paris, France.*
>
> *She rides outlaw horses, does anything a man can do astride a cantankerous mustang and has thrown more wild-eyed mavericks than the oldest "high-packing" "bye-there" broncho buster to be found from the plaza of El Paso to the plains of Moosejaw. She is simply "it" when it comes to sailing along on the back of a horse. She appears in the Robbins Bros. circus during the main performance and is an attractive figure at all times.*

At age fifty-one, she was characterized as

> *Lulu Bell Parr, famous lady bronc rider. Miss Parr is well known to Sioux Falls audiences, having appeared here a number of times in circuses and carnivals. She presents an attractive picture*

in the parades and through the show with her colorful costume. She is one of the hardest working members of the show, always on hand to take part in whatever is necessary.

Portrait of Lulu Bell Parr, n.d., by Frederick W. Glasier, American, 1866-1950. Black and white photography, copy from glass plate negative, 8x10 inches, Negative Number 31. Permission to reproduce from the Collection of The John and Mable Ringling Museum of Art Archives.

I Ain't Afraid

Tracy clowned on. After his time with Robbins ended, he centered his career in Iowa, diligently entertaining children and night clubbers with expert juggling, classic clown costumes, and comedy. He remarried but seemed to carry a tarnished torch of lingering feelings for Lulu. As late as 1957, he clowned in Flagstaff, Arizona alongside "Lulu Belle, the Wonder Bear."

STILL AT IT

Bellefontaine, Ohio
May 1929

Of all the ways to celebrate the first of May, in 1929 Ben Williams chose a jaunt to Bellefontaine, Ohio. Bellefontaine, home to about nine thousand souls, the town with the nation's first concrete street, was hosting the 101 Ranch Wild West show. Williams, a reporter for a Springfield, Ohio newspaper, traveled north from Springfield through thirty miles of flattish farmland and boldly presented himself to Zack Miller.

> *I've come up to Bellefontaine to see your Wednesday night performance, wander around the lot, mix in with the show people, ride back to Springfield on the show train, and then write a story about my adventures. That is if you will give me permission.*

The Wild West show was struggling. Zack, the last surviving Miller brother took the bait. He not only said, "Yes," but let the reporter use his stateroom on the train. He also bid his employee "Pinkie" to make some caviar sandwiches for the man.

I Ain't Afraid

Williams had a ball. He rubbed shoulders with the show people, chatted them up, and poked his nose in the "privilege" car where the performers ate and socialized. He enjoyed the caviar sandwiches and coffee.

The next day, he filed an envy-evoking story of his fine time with the Wild West show. He boasted of meeting "Red Sublette, world's champion cowboy clown, who rides a mule called "Spark Plug" and "Lulu Parr, rode bucking horses for Buffalo Bill and still at it." In the giveaway magazine for the show, Lulu Parr was listed as the leader of the cowgirls.

Red Sublett & "Spark Plug" Tex Austin's Rodeo Chicago 1927. Ralph R. Doubleday, 1927, photographic postcard. Bruce McCarroll Collection of the Bonnie & Frank McCarroll Rodeo Archives, Dickinson Research Center, National Cowboy & Western Heritage Museum. RC2006.076.240-2.

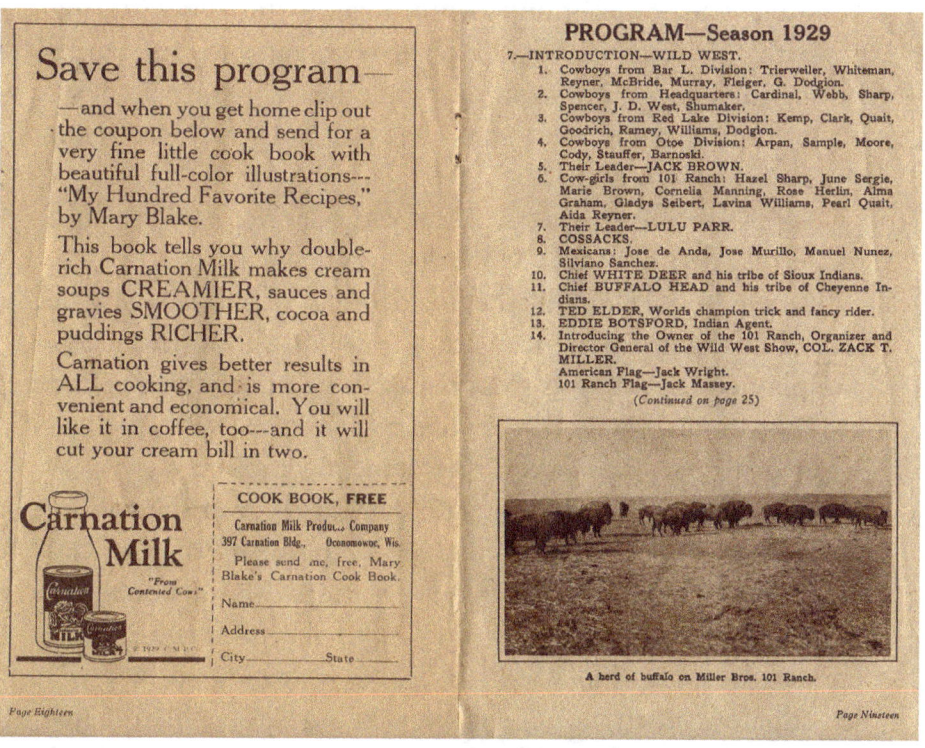

Miller Brothers Ranch 101 Wild West show Daily Review, 1929 Season, pages 18 and 19. Author's collection.

"Still at it" …at fifty-two, Lulu was a well-known pioneer Wild West performer. Yet, if anything, she was not slowing down or taking any shortcuts. Perhaps she sensed a change in the wind. Or felt a prickle up her spine of danger creeping up. That season, the end of the decade, the spring-through-fall of 1929, Lulu worked feverishly. She did not fiddle away her opportunities, like the laggard grasshopper in Aesop's fable. She was the ant, scuttling and scampering over the continent, laboring to prepare for the coming winter. She was everywhere.

I Ain't Afraid

Lulu had often hopped from show to show during performance seasons. For the prior few years, ads for Ponca Bill featured her as a headliner while nearly simultaneously planted publicity stories for the 101 Ranch touted her appearances with them.

The Greenough sisters, Alice and Margie, cowgirls and rodeo competitors from Montana, recalled Lulu performing with them in the King Brothers' rodeo that year. It was Margie and Alice's first experience with a traveling show. The sisters complained the pay was so poor that when the season ended in Des Moines, Iowa, all they had to show for their time was a can of tomato soup. With no traveling money, they were forced to stay in Des Moines and work there over the winter.

Ponca Bill's publicist still brayed in front page articles planted in newspapers, "She (Lulu) stands without a peer and is the highest salaried rider known to the profession." The unanswered question was "Compared to what? To whom?" Exactly how much money she was earning was not shared nor how low the bar was set for the other performers.

The end of the season was particularly frenetic for Lulu. On September 11, 1929, she was in Macon, Georgia as leader of the 101 Ranch Show's cowgirls, galloping into the arena with the cowboys, two tribes of Indians, Cossacks, and Colonel Zack T. Miller. A day later, an article in the *Cincinnati Enquirer* reported she was appearing with Jim Eskew's congress of cowboys and cowgirls at the city's cheesy amusement park, Coney Island. Eskew's troupe rode everything from bucking broncos to steers, mules, and American bison. Ten days later, she was scheduled to appear with Ponca Bill's Wild West in Dodge City, Kansas.

While Lulu wrapped up her work for the 1929 season, previously open windows began to close on her career —

unanticipated, beyond her control, and overwhelming. The death knell was ringing for women bronc riders.

The first sign of trouble was the loss of champion cowgirl Bonnie McCarroll on September 29. Lulu had worked with McCarroll over the years. An excellent bronc rider, McCarroll was the first winner of the bronc riding championship at Madison Square Garden. She won the Lord Selfridge Trophy at the British Empire Exhibition in 1925. In 1929, Bonnie and her cowboy husband Frank announced they were retiring from the rodeo life. But first, they would ride one last time at Oregon's Pendleton Rodeo. Rumor was Bonnie intended to put any prize money earned toward outfitting their new home in Boise, Idaho.

About one-third of all rodeos had female events at the time, but — based on misguided chivalry — women rode to different rules. At the British Empire Exhibition, for instance, women bronc riders were required to mount the horses in chutes, could use two reins, and "may use hobbles if desired." Men mounted in the arena or in chutes, only held one rein, and never used hobbles.

Hobbles. Binding the stirrups together under the horse's belly was seen as a crutch to make it easier for women to ride. The women could tuck their feet into the stirrups and keep them there, free of needing to contend with them flying about. The downside was that it made jumping off the horse more difficult. The top of the woman rider's foot could become wedged up against the stirrup or entangled in it. Men and many women rode "slick" — that is, free of hobbles.

Pendleton Rodeo rules in 1929 required women to ride hobbled. Bonnie McCarroll's bucker "Black Cat," according to a rodeo clown who witnessed the disaster, first flipped over backwards and crushed Bonnie. The horse next somersaulted forward, landed again on Bonnie, then began bucking. Bonnie was unconscious. When the pickup rider attempted to free her from the saddle, her foot caught in the hobbled stirrup. Eventually, after being bounced around the arena and repeatedly striking her head, Bonnie fell free. Her husband rushed in, carried her to an automobile, and drove her to the hospital. The thirty-four-year-old woman lingered for eleven days before dying, time used by the media to amplify the pathos of her final ride.

Rodeo officials had complained about the dangers of bronc riding for women for years. With Bonnie McCarroll's horrific death, women's bronc riding as a rodeo event collapsed. As the Rodeo Association of America was formed in 1929 to help organize the sport, women's rodeo events were not sanctioned. McCarroll's death was given as the rationale. Women competitors soon had only barrel racing open to them at Rodeo Association of America rodeos. That is, unless they want to compete for the title of rodeo pageant queen.

Lulu had not often, if ever, competed in rodeos. Instead, she typically rode as an exhibitor of the sport. But now, with the changes in the rodeo world, even those opportunities evaporated.

A month after McCarroll's death, on October 29, 1929, Wall Street crashed. Not only women's bronco riding but many other ways of life stumbled and fell away, never to recover. Doors slammed around the world.

DEJÀ VU

*Yellow Creek Township, Columbiana County, Ohio
April 30, 1930*

In April 1930, for the first time in thirty years, a US census enumerator found Lulu. Unlike all the other springs since 1903, Lulu was not gallivanting around with a traveling show. She was holed up in the hinterlands north of Steubenville.

Life was a throwback to earlier times — the days before she shook off life in an Ohio river town, before she hitched her star to Pawnee Bill, before she metamorphosized into a cowgirl. In 1903, Lulu had been renting a room from the Hipsley family when she left to become a Wild Wester. Maud and her husband, Benjamin Hipsley, lived over their Buckeye Sign Company on Fourth Street in Steubenville. That same year Maud gave birth to a baby boy she named Benjamin.

Once again, in 1930, Lulu was boarding with Maud. Lulu's latest divorce, from Tracy Andrews, had been filed four months earlier in Illinois and was pending resolution. Instead of a stuffy room over a print shop, she lived on the farm Maud had moved to in Columbiana County, north of Steubenville. Rather than live music from a cowboy band and the applause of excited crowds, birdsong, and moos along with scratchy radio music filled Lulu's ears.

Maud owned the farm and worked at home as a seamstress. Her mother and son lived there, too. Benjamin, single, was a salesman at the local feedstore. Fifty-six years old, Maud had divorced Benjamin Hipsley in 1907 and never remarried.

Lulu, two years younger than Maud, told the census enumerator she was thirty-eight and he dutifully recorded this as her age. She gave her occupation as a horsewoman in the Wild West industry and said she was unemployed. After decades of hitting the road in early spring with her fellow performers, she was stuck on a farm out in the boondocks of the Midwest.

In July, Lulu found a job. The "former woman bucking horse riding champion of the world…thrilled Battle Creek spectators" for a week in the Wild West portion of the D.D. Murphy show.

The D.D. Murphy show was embarrassingly small potatoes, but it was a job, nevertheless. The *Battle Creek Enquirer* described it as "A carnival…a composite of rides, freaks and vaudeville." The "minstrel show" had a skimpy cast of three tap dancers, a five-woman chorus, and a so-called "orchestra" with a whopping three instruments. A two-headed cow, and six and eight-footed horses were exhibited as freaks. Two new rides promised thrills and came with probably more danger than intended. One was the Leaping Lena, a rickety handful of metal topless sedans on a clearly collapsible circular course. The other was "the Waltzer, a device with whirling cars, the speed rising to a crescendo toward the latter half of the five minutes it continues."

Lulu was *the* feature of the Wild West show. A little thicker through the middle than in past years, she flashed a broad smile under her big hat in promotional photographs. For her outfit, she wore the old cowgirl classics — a floppy scarf tied in a bow across her chest, a fringed skirt, and tall, ornately embellished boots. The rest of the Wild West show consisted of a ten-year-old boy rope-spinner, the boy's partner, one "dancing" horse, a bucking mule, and "some Australian whip cracking" to round things out.

As the Depression deepened, Americans struggled. Lulu, like others, clawed out an existence and kept body and soul together. Barely.

BROTHER BILL

Steubenville, Ohio
June 1917

Over the years, while Lulu had cavorted on swirling, twirling pintos, buckskins, and palominos, her only sibling, William Alfred Parr, lived a quiet life. He and Dora divorced. In 1917, he married Emma W. Hoagland and became stepfather to her two young daughters, Naomi and Elsie. Emma was twenty-one.

They moved from Steubenville to Dayton, Ohio, a thriving center of industry and invention, with opportunities for a blue-collar laborer like Bill. Jobs were plentiful. Everything from cash registers to airplane parts were made in Dayton.

For a few years, the Parrs lived in rented houses. In March 1927, they bought a lot with a dollar down and a three-hundred-dollar mortgage. The north Dayton neighborhood, in Mad River township, was known as Little Rohr Farm. Later the area would become part of the small city of Riverside. Rural and impoverished, the neighborhood homes were lit with kerosene lamps. Sewage disposal was by outhouses. At one time, a single well served the entire area. One woman later recalled a family that moved in next door to the Parrs.

Diane Helentjaris

> "They just nailed down 2x4s and hung blankets over them. I remember I went home to my mama and said, "We are poor, but there are some people moving in down there who are poorer than we are."

Bill built a small house on his wooded lot at the corner of Rondowa and Pleasant Valley. A block away was Valley Road, a major artery linking Dayton with Springfield, thirty miles east, by following alongside the narrow Mad River. Bill's cabin, covered with green tarpaper, was topped with a pyramidal roof, and fronted by a tiny porch. Outside the backdoor was a handpump. In later years, the pump did not work, and truth be told, there is no documentation it ever did. The house had a dirt floor, no running water, no electricity, and no plumbing. "It was dark in there," said a neighbor.

Bill worked a variety of jobs, earning a living as a laborer and a sawyer. On August 19, 1931, he was employed at Leland Electric in Dayton when he fell through a skylight. Hospitalized with a hip injury, he never returned to his prior level of health or employability.

By 1933, Lulu had moved in with her brother's family. At fifty-six, she still considered herself a Wild West cowgirl. She burned to get back in the saddle, to perform, to hear the roar of an audience, and to smell a lathered-up bronco. She also needed the money.

In the autumn of 1933, a possible solution for Lulu rolled up, big as you please, right next door to Bill's house. The neighbor man's brother, a Walter Swain, was traveling down to Florida with his wife and nine-year-old stepson, Herbert. Behind their automobile, they pulled a trailer with a tent and baggage. When the Swains motored out of Dayton, Lulu went with them. Her "101 Ranch" trunks were tucked in the trailer. Mrs. Swain said, "The mister and I had always wanted to go south for the winter, so we decided we might as well strike out and try it. We stopped in Dayton and picked up Miss Parr, who lives next door to my husband's brother there."

The travelers made the front page of the *Lexington Herald-Leader* on October 25. Always a cooperative raconteur with the press, Lulu had entertained the reporter with tales of her Wild West career. As always, she lied about her age, claiming to be forty-one rather than fifty-six. Omitting her D.D. Murphy engagement, she said she had not performed since being injured in Memphis in 1929. Lulu's scheme was to drum up a job with Ringling Brothers – Barnum and Bailey Circus for the coming performance cycle by presenting herself at their Sarasota headquarters.

She also explained that to buy food and gasoline for the trip, she and Mr. Swain peddled soap door-to-door. They had pitched their tent just outside the Lexington, Kentucky city limits on the Old Frankfort Pike and planned to travel into Lexington to sell soap for a few more days, then head south. Mrs. Swain was in charge of keeping "house" and teaching her son his lessons, so he didn't fall behind in his schooling.

Lulu did not get work with the circus. Somehow, she made it back to Dayton.

She then sought work from her first employer, Pawnee Bill. Though Pawnee claimed to have given up on the Wild West touring circuit, he did continue to put on small shows while running his tourist-oriented trading post. Pawnee had retained the public's good will and continued to be the courtly, decent professional.

On March 22, 1934, he wrote Lulu a letter on his highly decorated sepia-and-brown "Pawnee Bill's Old Town and

Indian Trading Post" letterhead. He mailed it off to her at her brother's address.

Reverse side of Pawnee Bill's March 22, 1934, letter to Lulu Bell Parr. Author's collection.

Dear Miss Parr:
The show which I am sending out will have fifteen people with it and eleven head of horses. Mr. Bill Penny will go in charge and in talking with him this morning he tells me that he has two bucking horse riders engaged and therefore

can not consider hiring another as we only ride one bucker each performance. This is not a very big performance as it is a concert feature with the Harrington Nickle Plate Show.

Mrs. Lillie and I are both well and things are drifting along about as well as could be expected during these turbulent times.
With best wishes, I am
Your friend,
G.W. Lillie "Pawnee Bill"

PS. Tune in on KVCO, Tulsa, Oklahoma, 1140 kilocycles, 25,000 watts, 263.2 milometers, at 7:30 P.M. Central Standard Time, Wednesday, March 28. I will be on the air in a thirty minute courtesy broadcast. Listen in and then tell us what you think of it. GW

Her original mentor had turned her down as an employee. Politely and gently, but completely. True to his word, Pawnee Bill was scheduled as a guest speaker in a radio slot. In a letter to the *Wichita Eagle*, the showman explained,

During the time that my partner Cody and I had our show we made thousands of friends. Hardly a town that we appeared in but we met many of the most prominent citizens of the town.

But now I have been out of the show business for 21 years, since 1913. While I meet a few of them and hear from a few of them every year, many of my old friends, I presume, think I have passed over the Great Divide. Captain Payne, Kit

Carson and Buffalo Bill have, but such is not the case with me. I am living on my buffalo ranch at Oldtown, among my Indian friends, my buffalo, saddle horses, etc., and am running an old Indian trading post and meet all of my old Indian and western friends, but so few of my eastern friends get this far west that it gives me great pleasure to be able to send greetings to them. I am hale and hearty and enjoying myself as much as ever.

Next, on April 19, 1934, Tex Austin's Rodeo Headquarters in Fort Worth postmarked a letter to Lulu at Bill's house. Austin was pulling together a second rodeo in London at the White City. His troupe of cowboys and cowgirls planned to perform before the king and queen. The program's published rules for this event continued the gender differences. Women who competed in the bucking horse events, but not men, could use two reins and hobbles if they desired.

Six women bucking horse riders, including Alice Greenough, were featured in the printed program. Lulu was not among them and there is no evidence she participated. Most likely Austin's envelope contained a polite refusal to a request from Lulu to participate in the rodeo — another opportunity to earn a living, to be independent, gone.

Refusing to give up, in 1935, Lulu doggedly wrote directly to John Ringling at his circus's headquarters in Sarasota. Ringling kept the letter with its colorful envelope advertising Lulu's cowgirlhood, but no job was forthcoming.

The Depression inched on, relentless, grinding down hopes and dreams and lives.

On December 10, 1936, Lillian Kirkman's letter to Lulu was postmarked in El Centro, California. She mailed it to

I Ain't Afraid

Lulu in care of Bill Board in Cincinnati, the default address for many entertainers and performers. On January 16, the following year, the letter was postmarked again, the address scratched out, and sent to Lulu at her brother's home.

Lillian was William and Jennie Sheehan's daughter, Lulu's cousin whom she had lived with as a child. Since that time, Lillian had married, had a son, been widowed, remarried, and was living alone.

> *Dear Lula,*
>
> *Hope this won't surprise or shock you so your health will be impaired. If I wrote to you as often as I think of you my letters would become a nuisance.*
>
> *Looking through my small dictionary I found a card – Miss Lula Bell Parr – World's Champion Lady Bucking Bronco Rider – with Billie Burke Frontier Days. In Vaudeville, Season 1910-1911 Permanent address Bill Board.*
>
> *Bill Board – that's the idea, I don't know her address but that will always find her.*
>
> *Immediately I'll write a few lines – Mae said she wrote you after I came to Calif – but received no answer.*
>
> *One year this past September I came to Calif – I love it here in this state always have. I am working, have to – mighty lonesome but tell myself- there is something better coming. Have my off days and have thoughts of hurrying this life out – then I look around all so much beauty of nature – that the Supreme Being the unknown power provides for us I know my time is not yet.*
>
> *I may be staying here (on this earth) to see*

you again? Who knows. I was at the beach Ocean Beach (where Mae is staying) almost a year, taking care of children etc. but got no where.

Answered this ad for companion (was in San Diego paper) companion to elderly women. I say -it's do all the work there is to do. She has eighteen apartments and 7 (seven) sleeping rooms now don't see apartments as they are in the east but as they build them here – wood structure – on the ground flat and they are built on top, under, and hanging out on the sides, one room and kitchen maybe two rooms and kitchen, people come for week or two or longer away they go then that's my job to clean up, collect rent, write receipts, put in from twelve to seventeen hrs. day Sunday as any other day. Been here since Sep 4th. In all my life this is the hardest work I have ever did. Suppose I had to know now I didn't intend telling you this at all so that's enough…

If you receive this have time write and maybe I will write again Old lady is getting restless. Keeps talking to me so byby love and best things to you. LBK

RIVERSIDE REMEMBRANCES

Riverside neighborhood, Dayton, Ohio
1939

Life moved on for Lulu though Lulu did not budge. She stayed planted — tethered to Dayton by family, poverty, and a lack of work. The longest uninterrupted period of her life was spent at her brother Bill's humble home. After flitting about the world as a traveling performer, she had landed. She was one of the settled, the established onlookers.

Around 1939, a group of Romani moved into the neighborhood. They were squatters. The landowner repeatedly ousted them and told them they must buy land to live on it. Locals complained they "stole from everyone," and "stole everyone's chickens." On the other hand, "They had the prettiest bedspreads they'd hang out on the lines." How Lulu, as a former chronic rambler herself felt about them, is unknown.

In 1940, Lulu informed the census enumerator she was unemployed and unable to work. With no longer any reason to fib about her age — either to entice a job offer or a male admirer — she shared her real age, sixty-three years old, and her education level, third grade. She claimed to be a widow, though she had four living ex-husbands.

No one lives their lives unnoticed, including the Parrs. Over the years, spurred by Lulu's celebrity, neighbors divulged their observations to newspapers and local historians. Lulu, Bill, Emma, and Emma's daughters were knit into the fabric of the cluster of homes stretched parallel to the Mad River.

As a group, the Parrs "seemed like Christian people," but their religion was unknown. They were loners, "didn't talk much."

Bill was about five feet and ten inches tall, "chunky," "looked like Santa, all rounded." He worked as a traveling evangelist and junk dealer. He collected salvage, bought and sold tin cans, glass, and other scrap. At one time, he had a horse and wagon. He also owned an old Essex car.

"He never drove it nowhere, but he had it."

"Every now and then Bill would get in that black leather change purse of his and give me a penny for a Tootsie Roll."

His wife Emma was "heavy set and pretty. She had a big braid clear down her back. Looked kind of Amish." Emma was thought to be diabetic, and at one time in the 1940s, had been bedridden for a year or two.

Lulu's hair was "kind of gray but had blond through it."

"Her hair looked like straw color."

She had a wig and told the children she was scalped by the Indians. She didn't smoke. Nothing was known about any husbands of hers. Lulu had a big Bible.

She also owned firearms — several pistols and at least two breach and block rifles. Her guns were well-known in the neighborhood. Lulu discussed her desire to leave them to the local constable Bill Jones as he "often stopped in and talked with the ladies." Her weaponry included the pearl-handled colt given to her in 1911 by Buffalo Bill Cody and engraved "To Lulu from Buffalo Bill." Another was described as diamond-encrusted.

Robert Gamble was a Riverside village marshal in 1953.

> *I was riding with Constable Carl Coomer when he got a call to go (to) her house. Someone had threatened her or was trying to break in. When we got there, she was standing out there with a "hog leg," which is a frontier revolver. She was standing there with these great big ol' guns that were as big as she was. She was a feisty little lady.*

Audrey Shade, a Riverside resident who walked by Lulu's home when she came home from school, recalled,

> *I remember seeing her out sitting around under the trees and talking to everyone. She did talk to everyone, showing pictures of her and telling what she used to be in the rodeo. She had this trunk with old costumes in it.*

Lulu would sit and wait for the children's school bus in the afternoon, wearing a big sombrero, ready to entertain them with tales from her earlier times. She told the children she "was a real Wild West star," "told the neighborhood children about her trips to England when she was with the Wild West shows," and showed her old photographs around at the grocery store and to her neighbors.

"Lulu was a good and kind person."

Clara Ankeny Blair's parents also lived on Rondowa and were friends with the Parrs.

> *She was a very sweet lady. She wasn't afraid of*

*anything — she'd even walk her dog at midnight.
She said she could handle a gun and I remember
her saying, "I got to prove that I could handle
a gun."*

Others, too, mentioned Lulu often walking her dogs late at night, between midnight and about 2:30 a.m., dressed in a coat and scarf.

"I'd say when the dishes got washed, the dogs done it. They were good people, but not tidy."

In December 1949, Bill Parr died at age seventy-eight of pneumonia. His stepdaughter Naomi had married years earlier. Soon Elsie would move out, too. She was in a relationship with Harry Montague who owned a junk shop on Valley Pike. "Harry Montague wore that slickum on his hair. He was a crook and would crook you anytime he could."

Lulu and her sister-in-law Emma were left on their own in the house built by Bill on Rondowa.

*(They) loved kids and dogs. They never bothered
anybody. They just wanted to be left alone. But
they always seemed to be happy that way.*

FETCHING THE WATER

Riverside neighborhood, Dayton, Ohio
1954

As the autumn of 1954 moved into winter, life went on for Lulu and Emma. Though twenty years older, Lulu had long been the more active of the pair. A stroke paralyzing Emma's right side had made the lopsidedness of their partnership permanent.

Bill's house had edged into shack-dom. The women shared it with four dogs and at least one cat. Lulu kept her memorabilia, newspaper clippings, photographs, postcards, letters, mementos, sombreros, hats, costumes, and guns from her Wild West days, piled high in a small room.

Lulu was destitute. She received what was euphemistically labeled a "pension" from the Montgomery County Division of Aid, general welfare, but it wasn't enough money for her to be well-nourished. She was skinny. She most likely suffered significant traumatic arthritis from her cowgirl-related injuries and fractures. Her body bore the true and escalating cost of those glamorous trips to London, Paris, and Rio de Janeiro.

The women bought groceries from a man named Johnny Meyers who owned a grocery store around the corner. The only source of water for the two women was a neighborhood gas station. Shaped like a windmill, it added a dash of quirky midcentury style to Valley Pike. The owner, Charles Peifer, looked the other way when Lulu filled her bucket from his tap. Unless Lulu walked the block or so to the gas station and brought water home, there was nothing to wet a washcloth, make tea, or drink.

Winter came as it always does. Lulu fell early in the week of January 10th, 1955, toting a bucket of water home. Shortly after, she apparently had a stroke. Or maybe she had the stroke and then fell. The answer to that is lost. Either way, injured, she gathered her strength as she had so many times before. The seventy-eight-year-old made it across her threshold.

The two women stayed in their house, even though Lulu fell off the davenport onto the floor on Saturday, helpless. Emma was unable to lift and move her. The pair, terrified they would be institutionalized in the Montgomery County Home, didn't call for help.

Eventually, a pastor realized they had not been seen for several days. Lulu, semi-conscious and moaning, was taken on Sunday, January 16 to Miami Valley Hospital down in Dayton. Emma, in poorer shape than usual after attempting to care for herself and Lulu, also was admitted to the same hospital.

On Monday, January 17, 1955, at 11:30 p.m. Lulu Bell Parr died, sixteen hours after being admitted to the hospital. She had not regained consciousness.

The media quickly sniffed out Lulu's past as a celebrity, a star, blazing across the world of Wild West shows and rodeos. The day after her death, her story was on the front page of both of Dayton's papers, the *Journal Herald* and *Dayton Daily News*. The *Journal Herald* noted,

I Ain't Afraid

One of her best acts was shooting glass balls from the backs of horses with a .45. Her other trick riding and sharpshooting acts reportedly pleased audiences throughout the United States, England, and South America.

Illustrating the story were photographs of her cat sitting on a bare mattress amid a pile of junk, one of her dogs being carried by the scruff of its neck by a humane society worker, and of the tumbled-down tarpaper shack she'd called home.

The *Dayton Daily News* described her as "a neighborhood legend." The AP wire service spread the word across the nation about her "glittering past" and the sad circumstances of her final days.

On her death certificate, Lulu's cause of death was listed as a stroke, with malnutrition as a contributing factor. Harry Montague provided the information. Her occupation was listed as "housewife" and her marital status as "widow."

On the morning of January 21, the Reverend William H. Boyer conducted Lulu's funeral service. He had also preached at her brother Bill's funeral. Pastor Boyer spoke of "Lula," the endearment used by those close to her.

In 1912, Pastor Boyer had founded the Dayton Brethren in Christ Mission church in the poorest section of the city, the only Dayton neighborhood Lulu and Bill would ever live in. Known for his integrity, compassion, and service, Pastor Boyer taught others "that to be truly human one must serve." He is most likely the minister who realized Lulu had not been seen after her fall.

After Pastor Boyer's service, Lulu Bell Parr was buried in an unmarked grave in the Mennonite Cemetery in Medway. The cemetery lay less than a dozen miles up Valley Pike from

Rondowa Avenue.

Lulu died a pauper, without a will, and, by probate court mathematics, could not afford her own death. Lulu's sole assets were two Colt forty-five revolvers worth thirty-five dollars and they were in the custody of the Sheriff. Whether the court costs, attorney fees, and funeral expenses totaling $325 were ever paid is not documented. The Department of Public Welfare appears to have been stuck with the bill for her burial. Even with the newspaper articles' uproar over her death, no one stepped up to provide a tombstone.

Spring warmed the soil and tractors rumbled across the nearby fields. Grass grew over the scar of Lulu Bell Parr's burial. The grass was cut by the caretaker, watered by booming and clattering summer thunderstorms, and recut over and over. By autumn, no one could tell a coffin lay beneath the lush sod.

EPILOGUE

Medway, Ohio
2000

Like many in the closing months of the 20th century, family history fascinated Larry and Floyd Parr. The Parr brothers wondered if they were related to Wild West performer Lulu Bell Parr. They were aware of Lulu's family ties with Pennsylvania and, though they lived in other states, knew they had forebears from Pennsylvania. Sleuthing about, they discovered she was buried in Ohio, possibly in Medway.

The men contacted the Montgomery County Historical Society and were referred to the Medway Area Historical Society. No one in Medway knew anything about Lulu Bell Parr, but the Society members were intrigued. Neither Lulu Bell Parr nor her brother was listed in a book put together with the readings of the cemetery. The Society contacted the Medway Cemetery Association. Cemetery records confirmed Lulu's burial in the Medway Cemetery as well as that of her brother Bill and his wife Emma. All three were buried in unmarked graves.

The local history folks sprang into action. Delving deep into burial records, they confirmed Lulu had been buried in the Medway Cemetery. In December 2000, Lulu's grave was located on the east side of the cemetery. Nancy Brown, President of the Medway Area Historical Society, and Dixie Gergal went to the Dayton Metro Public Library to search for her obituary. Later, Dixie Gergal went to the Montgomery County Courthouse to get a copy of her death certificate and to search probate records. Dixie and Nancy, along with Connie Moore, Scott Suther, and his brother Dave researched Lulu.

Marcia Walgren, owner of the Ohio Silver Company jewelry shop in nearby Yellow Springs, also assisted. She was a circus fan. In the 1970s, she discovered a cache of Lulu Bell's personal memorabilia at a Springfield flea market. Walgren bought a collection of the photographs and postcards. Later, she donated copies of some of these to the Medway Area Historical Society. The two Parr brothers, though they turned out not be kin, also found Lulu Bell Parr irresistible and pitched in to help.

Usual genealogic sources were scoured for information about Lulu. Scott Suther traveled to New Cadiz to scan gravestone inscriptions and cemetery records for possible information about Lulu's family, drove to Fort Wayne to see what records were available at Lulu's birthplace, and went to Steubenville to look through public records. He located her divorce decree from George Barrett.

To find out as much as possible, the team reached out to folks who might know something about her. They contacted descendants of Emma Parr's daughters. Not every effort was fruitful as Scott found out when a descendant of one of Lulu's husbands hung up on him.

The Medway historians collaborated with the Riverside Historical Society. Nancy, Dixie, and Scott spent a bit of shoe leather canvassing Lulu's old neighborhood. They met and interviewed people who remembered her and her family. This information was typed up and retained as a reference.

Scott, using personal funds and his vacation time, traveled out west — way out west, past Indiana and Illinois, across the Mississippi River.

> *I've always liked the West and stuff, so once we found out about her, I planned my vacation around researching her...Everywhere I went, I took [material] with me. And I left material everywhere I went, so I was kind of building up their collections, too...To me, history is for everybody.*

He visited sites he felt might have information about the Wild West performer – the Pawnee Bill Museum in Oklahoma, the Frontier Days Museum in Cheyenne, the Buffalo Bill Grave and Museum in Colorado, and others.

Convinced Lulu deserved a marked grave, the Medway Area Historical Society members hunkered down to raise money to pay for one. Regional newspapers covered the story. The group placed ads in magazines popular with fans of the Old West and asked for donations. They collected aluminum cans and turned them in for cash.

On March 24, 2001, the society hosted a Western Roundup Dinner fundraiser. Tickets went for five dollars if purchased ahead of time or six dollars at the door. The response was "overwhelming and money came from all over the United States." More than seven thousand dollars total was raised — enough for a tombstone for Emma and Bill as well as a monument for Lulu.

On September 15, 2001, a sunny midwestern Saturday, an excited throng paraded along Main Street in Medway, out to where it became Lower Valley Pike, and walked into the cemetery. School children, the Indian Creek Regulators reenactors, Lulu's prior neighbors, Medway residents, historians, horses, and a couple of burros sashayed down the middle of the road. Finally, they reached the Medway Cemetery, as the old Mennonite Cemetery is now known. A cloud of American flags surrounded the sixty-inch monument and flapped in the breeze. A ceremony dedicated it with speakers ranging from Nancy Brown, president of the historical society, to children from the nearby elementary schools.

Reenactors ride through Medway, Ohio on September 15, 2001, for the dedication of Lulu Bell Parr's monument in the Medway Cemetery. Courtesy of Scott Suther.

I Ain't Afraid

Local — *New Carlisle Sun, Wednesday, Sept. 19, 2001 - 3A*

Lulu Belle gets a long awaited tribute

Jennica Stout/Sun photos

Medway Historical Society hosted a special dedication to Lulu Belle Parr who was a member of the Buffalo Bill's Rodeo years ago. Her grave was unmarked in Medway Cemetery. When she was found to be buried there by a local historian they began fundraising efforts to get her a proper marker. Saturday the group celebrated with a parade including rope lassoing cowboys.

Clipping from *New Carlisle Sun*, Wednesday, September 19, 2001. Courtesy of Medway Area Historical Society.

The Medway historians were not finished. They had another goal. They believed Lulu deserved to be inducted into the National Cowgirl Hall of Fame in Fort Worth, Texas. In 2004, Scott submitted, on behalf of the society, an application for Lulu which was denied as it was too late for that year's consideration. Undeterred, Scott and his team put together a second nomination in 2005. He still recalls the moment he came home from work on June 15 and found a message on his answering machine. She was accepted!

On October 27, 2005, Scott was called to the stage at the

Diane Helentjaris

National Cowgirl Hall of Fame induction event.

> *I looked forward but only saw bright lights shining in my eyes. That was good because I didn't have to look at the 750 plus people in the audience.*

He accepted a plaque and medallion on Lulu's behalf.

Scott Suther with medal and plaque from induction of Lulu Bell Parr into the National Cowgirl Hall of Fame in 2005.
Courtesy of Scott Suther.

Scott continued to research Lulu. One day, he created a post about Lulu Bell Parr for the Medway Area Historical Association's social media site. The photo of the cowgirl caught my eye and I read Scott's summary. I was ensnared by her story and so began my quest to understand her part in history.

☆☆☆

Nothing much has changed in Medway since the summer day I ran away from home. Children swat baseballs in the diamonds across from my childhood ranch house. Down Gerlaugh Road, Copey's Butcher Shop sells sweet hams and dried beef. Timothy grass edges the fence lines at the Medway Cemetery, a quiet and peaceful place. Lulu Bell Parr rests under a monument bearing an etching of her in a cowgirl hat, smiling.

Lulu Bell Parr grave and monument, Medway Cemetery, Medway, Ohio. 2021 photograph by author.

Diane Helentjaris

I like to imagine a ghostly Lulu rising up in the darkness. She glides over to an apparition of the old stable where buggy horses awaited the Mennonites worshipping in the brick church. Lulu leads out a phantom sorrel and hops on its bare back for a ride – a one-woman parade down Main Street. Young and lithe, Lulu waves and smiles to the spirits of the children, women, and men crowding the sidewalk. At Sycamore and Main, she toes the sorrel. He rears up, whinnies. With a gloved hand, she swoops her sombrero in a wide arc. Lulu Bell Parr is ecstatic.

I Ain't Afraid

Portrait of Lulu Bell Parr, n.d., by Frederick W. Glasier, American, 1866-1950. Black and white photography, copy from glass plate negative, 8x10 inches, Negative Number 134. Permission to reproduce from the Collection of The John and Mable Ringling Museum of Art Archives.

ACKNOWLEDGMENTS

Many have been kind and generous with their time and skills as I put this book together. I want to thank all of you.

Scott Suther first brought Lulu to my attention. Scott's dedication to local history is phenomenal. He has shown us all how a small "unincorporated community and census-designated place" like Medway can hold historic treasure. Always willing to help and share, Scott was the linchpin for this project. He pointed me to other helpful and informative souls, especially Dan Katz and Marcia Walgren.

Brenda S. Applegate and Tony Keiser of the Beaver County Historical Research and Landmark Foundation as well as the Beaver County Genealogy and History Center gave pivotal information about Lulu's family in Pennsylvania. Surprisingly, part of this story is rooted right here in Leesburg, Virginia where I live. Alexandra Gressitt, Laura Christiansen, and the Thomas Balch Library supported my efforts to learn about this. Natalie Fritz of Clark County, Ohio's Heritage Center helped run down a research dead-end. The John and Mable Ringling Museum of Art and the Denver Public Library donated important tools to this project.

Family pitched in and helped. As always, my brother Greg Helentjaris gave insight, listened, talked, and dug up Dayton records. I especially appreciate Lorena, my sister-in-law, spending hours looking at funky microfiche in Dayton. My cousins weren't spared. Melissa Helentjaris put me in touch with Renice Gray. Marcia Helentjaris — a distant relative of Buffalo Bill — pointed me to other resources. My husband has listened patiently to hours (or more honestly, days) of me reading draft versions to him. And with no complaints. My son Nick is my office assistant, my barista, my photo editor, and buddy.

Getting this project up and humming depended on the Hellenic Writers' Group of Washington, DC, especially its Critique Group. For months, they read about Lulu and shared their insights, thoughts, and recommendations. Thanks to Stratis Aloimonos, Ipatia Apostolides, Ph.D., Sharon Blomfield, Maria A. Karamitsos, Stella Lagakos, Aphrodite Pallas, Andie Petrides, Ann Podaras, and Marigo J. Stathis.

My beta readers are the best! Each gave important feedback. Thanks to John I. Brown III, Renice Gray, Gwen Miller, Linda H. Sittig, and Scott Suther. Sheila Ralph, Ph.D., gave input as well.

John DeDakis was a pleasure as editor. Tahlia Newland and Rose Newland are such a wonderful combination of skills, energy, competence, and fun. I am lucky to work with them to get this book out and into readers' hands.

I am responsible for any errors. The opinions expressed as narrator are mine alone. Much of Lulu Bell Parr's life story remains to be studied. It's tucked away in scrapbooks, attics, unpublished diaries, and oral histories. I look forward to its emergence.

BIBLIOGRAPHY

Books

Abel, Richard. 2006. *Americanizing the Movies and "Movie-Mad" Audiences, 1910 - 1914*. Berkeley, Los Angeles, London: University of California Press.

Arty, Allen, and James Willard Mace. 2017. *Jess Willard: Heavyweight Champion of the World (1915 – 1919)*. Jefferson, North Carolina: McFarland.

Bricklin, Julia. 2017. *America's Best Female Sharpshooter: The Rise and Fall of Lillian Frances Smith (Volume 2) (William F. Cody Series on the History and Culture of the American West)*. Norman, Oklahoma: University of Oklahoma Press.

Clement, Samuel Spottford. 2009. *Memoirs of Samuel Spottford Clement*. Edited by Sara Ovington. Wokingham, UK: Dodo Press.

Enss, Chris. 2006. *Buffalo Gals: Women of Buffalo Bill's Wild West Show*. Helena, Montana: TwoDot Books.

Enss, Chris. 2010. *Many Loves of Buffalo Bill*. Helena, Montana: TwoDot Books.

Farnum, Allen L. 1992. *Pawnee Bill's Historic Wild West: A Photo Documentary of the 1900-05 Show Tours*. West Chester, Pennsylvania: Schiffer Publishing Ltd.

Galperin, Patricia O. 2012. *In Search of Princess White Deer: A Biography*. Sparta, NJ: Flint & Feather Press.

Haefeli, Evan, and Kevin Sweeney. 2006. *Captive Histories: English, French, and Native Narratives of the 1704 Deerfield Raid*. Amherst and Boston: University of Massachusetts Press.

James, Monica. 2006. *Buckskin Bessie: Her Lost Letters*. Glendale, Arizona: Buckskin Press.

LeCompte, Mary Lou. 2000. *Cowgirls of the Rodeo: Pioneer Professional Athletes*. Urbana and Chicago: University of Illinois Press.

Marvine, Dee. 2005. *The Lady Rode Bucking Horses: The Story of Fannie Sperry Steele, Woman of the West*. Helena, Montana: TwoDot Books.

Pearl, Matthew. 2021. *The Taking of Jemima Boone: Colonial Settlers, Tribal Nations, and the Kidnapping That Shaped America*. New York: HarperCollins Publishers.

Ronnie, Art. 1995. *Counterfeit Hero: Fritz Duquesne, Adventurer and Spy*. Annapolis, Maryland: Naval Institute Press.

Rosa, Joseph G., and Robin May. 1989. *Buffalo Bill and His Wild West*. Lawrence, Kansas: University Press of Kansas.

Sayers, Isabelle S. 1981. *Annie Oakley and Buffalo Bill's Wild West*. New York: Dover Publications.

Slide, Anthony. 2006. *New York City Vaudeville (NY) Images of America.* Mount Pleasant, South Carolina. Arcadia Publishing.

Tilghman, Zoe A. 1926. *Outlaw Days: A True history of Early-Day Oklahoma Characters, Revised and Enlarged from the Records of Wm. Tilghman.* Oklahoma City. Harlow Publishing Company.

Turnbaugh, Kay. 2009. *The Last of the Wild West Cowgirls: A True Story.* Nederland, Colorado: Perigo Press.

Turner, Erin, ed. *Cowgirls: Stories of Trick Riders, Sharp Shooters, and Untamed Women.* Helena, Montana: TwoDot Books.

Wallis, Michael. 1999. *The Real Wild West: The 101 Ranch and the Creation of the American West.* New York: St. Martin's Griffin.

Wetmore, Helen Cody. 1994. *Buffalo Bill: Last of the Great Scouts.* Stamford, Connecticut: Longmeadow Press.

Wilcox, Frank N., William McGill, et al. 2015. *Ohio Indian Trails: Third Edition.* Kent, Ohio: The Kent State University Press.

Zesch, Scott. 2004. *The Captured: A True Story of Abduction by Indians on the Texas Frontier.* New York: St. Martin's Griffin.

Dissertations and Theses

Koch, Iris. "Zack Mulhall, His Family, and the Mulhall Wild West Show." Master of Arts thesis, Oklahoma Agricultural and Mechanical College, 1940. (https://hdl.handle.net/11244/46403).

Moreno, Gary. "Charro: The Transnational History of a Cultural Icon."

Doctoral dissertation, University of Oklahoma, 2014. (https://hdl.handle.net/11244/10389).

Scofield, Rebecca Elena. 2015. "Riding Bareback: Rodeo Communities and the Construction of American Gender, Sexuality, and Race in the Twentieth Century." Doctoral dissertation, Harvard University, Graduate School of Arts & Sciences.

Taunton, Carla Jane. "Performing Resistance/Negotiating Sovereignty: Indigenous Women's Performance Art in Canada." PhD diss., Queen's University, Kingston, Ontario, 2011. (https://qspace.library.queensu.ca/items/242d8225-6218-47f3-afc3-a4a3778e9add/full).

ABOUT THE AUTHOR

Diane Helentjaris explores the lives of the unsung in her writing. She is the author of the novel *The Indenture of Ivy O'Neill* and was a 2020 finalist for the Iceland Writers' Retreat Alumni Award. Diane earned her BA cum laude in Interdisciplinary Humanities from Michigan State. As she grew up in Dayton and Medway, Ohio, she listened to her grandmother's tales. Her grandma was a descendent of a Native American woman and a man who rode in the Pony Express and someone back then was in a Wild West show, too. Diane believed it all. www.DianeHelentjaris.com.

www.ingramcontent.com/pod-product-compliance
Lightning Source LLC
Chambersburg PA
CBHW070505120526
44590CB00013B/750